I0478006

Understanding Your RIGHTS at Work

A Comprehensive Employee Guide to Discrimination in the Workplace

Understanding Your RIGHTS at Work

A Comprehensive Employee Guide to Discrimination in the Workplace

Jana Lomax, J.D.

Civil Rights Lawyer and Investigator

Understanding Your Rights at Work – A Comprehensive Employee Guide to Discrimination in the Workplace

Copyright © 2024 by Jana Lomax, J.D.

All rights reserved.

Fb.com/janallomaxjd

All characters and events portrayed in this book are fictitious. Any similarity to real persons, living or dead, is coincidental and not intended by the author.

No part of this book may be reproduced in any form or by any means without express written permission of the author.

ISBN-13: 9798345578124

Printed in the United States of America

Legal Disclaimer: The content of this book is for informational purposes only and should not be construed as legal advice. While the book provides valuable insights into discrimination law, it does not establish an attorney-client relationship between the author and the reader. I am not responsible for any actions taken (or not taken) based on the information provided in the book.

Each legal situation is unique, and the information in this book may not apply to your specific circumstances. For personalized legal advice, you should consult a qualified attorney. I disclaim any liability for any outcomes resulting from the use of the information in this book. All content is provided "as is" and I make no representations about the accuracy, completeness, or timeliness of the information. Only a licensed attorney can provide tailored advice that is appropriate to your situation.

Thank you for using this book as a resource, but please remember it's not a substitute for professional legal counsel.

To everyone who's faced discrimination at work: your courage in the face of adversity lights the way for change. Your stories matter, your voices deserve to be heard, and your resilience is the foundation of a more just and inclusive future. This book is for you—may it stand as a tribute to your strength and a rallying cry for a world where every workplace honors and respects the dignity of every person.

Never be afraid to raise your voice for honesty and truth and compassion against injustice and lying and greed. If people all over the world would do this, it would change the earth."

— William Faulkner

Table of Contents

Introduction

Understanding Your Rights at Work: A Comprehensive Employee Guide to Discrimination in the Workplace

In today's increasingly diverse and dynamic work environments, the issue of workplace discrimination has never been more relevant. **"Understanding Your Rights at Work"** is designed to be a vital resource for employees who wish to navigate the complexities of discrimination and advocate for their rights. This guide seeks to empower you by providing a clear understanding of workplace discrimination, the legal protections available to you, and practical steps you can take when facing these challenges.

Purpose of the Book

Importance of Understanding Workplace Discrimination

Workplace discrimination can manifest in various forms—ranging from subtle microaggressions to overt acts of bias—impacting hiring, promotions, compensation, and overall job satisfaction. Recognizing these signs is crucial, as many employees may not even realize they are facing discrimination until it significantly affects their career trajectory and mental health. By understanding the various types of discrimination—such as those based on race, gender, age, disability, sexual orientation, and religion—you will be better equipped to identify and address these issues in your workplace.

Empowering Employees with Knowledge of Their Rights

Knowledge is empowerment. Familiarity with your legal rights is essential for protecting yourself and advocating for fair treatment. This book breaks down the complex legal framework surrounding workplace discrimination, including federal and state laws, and explains how they apply to your specific situation.

In addition to legal protections, **"Understanding Your Rights at Work"** emphasizes the importance of personal empowerment. By equipping yourself with information about your rights, you can navigate your workplace with greater confidence. This guide offers practical advice on how to document incidents of discrimination, report them effectively, and what to expect from the investigation process.

More importantly, you will learn that you are not alone. The book provides insights into the supportive resources available, from employee assistance programs to legal aid, enabling you to seek help when needed.

In the chapters that follow, you will encounter a wealth of information, including comprehensive insights, actionable strategies, and real-world examples that illustrate how to recognize, confront, and report workplace discrimination. Through this knowledge, you can advocate for yourself and your colleagues, fostering a culture of inclusivity and respect in your workplace.

Ultimately, **"Understanding Your Rights at Work"** is more than just a guide—it's a call to action. Together, we can work towards creating a more equitable, supportive, and just work environment for all employees. By standing up for your rights and supporting others, you contribute to a workplace culture that values diversity, equity, and inclusion.

Overview of Workplace Discrimination

Workplace discrimination remains a critical issue affecting employees across various industries. It not only harms individuals but also has far-reaching consequences for workplace culture and organizational effectiveness. Understanding the prevalence and impact of discrimination is essential for fostering a fair and inclusive work environment.

Statistics on Discrimination in Various Industries

Discrimination can manifest in various forms and is prevalent in different sectors. Here are some key statistics that illustrate the scope of the problem:

- **General Statistics:**
  - The Equal Employment Opportunity Commission (EEOC) reported over 61,000 discrimination charges filed in a recent year, indicating that workplace discrimination is an ongoing concern.
  - The most frequently reported claims included retaliation (55.8%), which occurs when an employee is punished for asserting their rights, followed by race discrimination (36.7%) and sex discrimination (32.3%). These figures highlight that employees are often at risk for backlash when they speak out against unfair treatment.

- **Industry-Specific Data:**

- o **Technology Sector:** The technology industry continues to grapple with significant disparities in representation. Women hold only about 26% of computing jobs, and women of color are even less represented. This lack of diversity not only impacts hiring but also influences innovation and creativity within the field.

- o **Healthcare:** Research indicates that healthcare professionals from marginalized backgrounds frequently encounter bias in hiring and promotions. This discrimination can lead to disparities in leadership roles and negatively affect patient care due to a lack of diverse perspectives.

- o **Education:** Data from the National Center for Education Statistics shows that only about 20% of teachers in K-12 education identify as non-white. This underrepresentation can affect student outcomes and perpetuate systemic biases within the education system.

- o **Hospitality and Retail:** These industries have reported high instances of gender and racial discrimination, particularly in customer service roles. Employees in these sectors often experience hostile work environments, leading to high turnover rates and employee dissatisfaction.

The Impact of Discrimination on Employees and Workplace Culture

The effects of workplace discrimination extend beyond the individual level, influencing the broader organizational landscape. Here are some ways in which discrimination impacts both employees and workplace culture:

- **Individual Impact:**

  - o **Mental Health:** Employees who experience discrimination often report elevated levels of stress, anxiety, and depression. The psychological toll of facing bias can lead to burnout and a sense of isolation, making it difficult for affected individuals to perform at their best.

  - o **Career Advancement:** Discrimination can create barriers to career progression, with marginalized employees often facing fewer opportunities for promotions, raises, and professional development. This can perpetuate cycles of inequality and limit the overall diversity of leadership within organizations.

- o **Job Performance:** The constant stress of navigating a discriminatory work environment can detract from an employee's focus and motivation. This may result in decreased productivity, increased absenteeism, and a higher likelihood of turnover.

- **Organizational Impact:**

  - o **Workplace Culture:** A culture that tolerates or ignores discrimination fosters an environment of fear and mistrust. This can lead to lower employee morale and decreased collaboration among teams, ultimately hindering organizational performance and innovation.

  - o **Reputation:** Companies known for discriminatory practices may face public backlash, which can damage their brand and reputation. This not only affects current employee retention but also complicates efforts to attract diverse talent in the future.

  - o **Legal Consequences:** Organizations that fail to address discrimination may find themselves facing costly legal battles, settlements, and potential regulatory fines. The financial and reputational costs of discrimination can divert resources away from employee development and other critical initiatives.

In summary, workplace discrimination is a pervasive issue that poses significant challenges for both individuals and organizations. By understanding the statistics and recognizing the profound effects of discrimination, employees can be better equipped to advocate for themselves and push for necessary changes in their workplaces. Employers, on the other hand, must acknowledge these realities and commit to creating inclusive environments that prioritize equity and respect. This foundational knowledge sets the stage for the actionable strategies and insights that will be discussed in the subsequent chapters of this guide, empowering readers to take meaningful steps toward combating discrimination in their workplaces.

How to Use This Guide

"Understanding Your Rights at Work: A Comprehensive Employee Guide to Discrimination in the Workplace" is crafted to be an indispensable resource for employees, whether you're facing discrimination or simply aiming to educate yourself about your rights. This guide is structured for ease of use, enabling you to find the information you need quickly and effectively. Here's how to navigate the content and make the most of the resources included.

Navigating the Chapters

The book is thoughtfully organized into a series of chapters, each dedicated to a specific aspect of workplace discrimination. Here's how to effectively navigate through the chapters:

- **Chapter Summaries:** Each chapter begins with a concise summary that outlines the key topics covered. These summaries provide an overview of what to expect, allowing you to quickly identify areas that are particularly relevant to your situation or concerns.

- **Subsections for Clarity:** Within each chapter, information is further broken down into subsections that tackle specific issues. For instance, you might find subsections detailing various types of discrimination (e.g., racial, gender, age), as well as discussions on legal definitions and protections. This structure makes it easier to locate the exact information you need without wading through unrelated content.

- **Real-Life Examples:** Throughout the guide, real-life scenarios illustrate how discrimination has manifested in the workplace and the various strategies employed by individuals to address it. These examples provide context and relatability, helping you understand how the principles discussed can be applied in real-world situations.

- **Action Steps:** At the conclusion of each chapter, you will find a list of actionable steps you can take. These steps are designed to empower you with practical advice on how to advocate for your rights effectively, whether that means reporting discrimination, gathering evidence, or seeking support from colleagues or legal professionals.

Resources and Support Tools Included

This guide is packed with powerful resources and tools to help you take control of your workplace rights and take action against discrimination with confidence:

- **Legal Glossary**: A no-nonsense glossary of key legal terms related to workplace discrimination. Whether you're talking to HR, a lawyer, or dealing with formal proceedings, this glossary ensures you're speaking the same language and know exactly what's at stake.

- **Sample Templates**: Ready-to-use templates for reporting discrimination to HR, documenting incidents, and filing complaints. These templates are designed to make sure your concerns are communicated clearly and professionally, so you can make your voice heard and your case stronger.

- **Resource Directory**: A curated list of top organizations, advocacy groups, and government agencies that can offer legal support and advice. Whether you need local or national resources, this directory helps you connect with the right people to back you up.

- **Self-Assessment Tools**: A set of practical tools to help you evaluate your experiences and spot potential discrimination. With checklists and reflection questions, these tools guide you through documenting incidents, identifying patterns, and preparing for conversations with HR or legal professionals.

- **Hotlines and Support Services**: Direct access to hotlines and mental health resources to ensure you have emotional and practical support when you need it most. Facing discrimination can be tough, but you don't have to go it alone.

These resources aren't just about knowledge—they're about giving you the tools, support, and confidence to stand up for your rights, fight for justice, and take control of your workplace experience.

By utilizing the structured format and the wealth of resources included in this guide, you can confidently navigate the complexities of workplace discrimination. Whether you seek to better understand your rights, take meaningful action against discrimination, or support colleagues who may be experiencing bias, **"Understanding Your Rights at Work"** is designed to empower you at every step of your journey. With this guide in hand, you are equipped to foster a more equitable workplace for yourself and your peers, championing the incredibly important values of equality, inclusion, and respect within your organization.

Chapter 1: Understanding Discrimination

1.1　Definition of Workplace Discrimination

Discrimination is the unjust or prejudicial treatment of individuals or groups based on characteristics such as race, ethnicity, sex, sexual orientation, gender identity, age, disability, religion, or other attributes. It encompasses a range of behaviors and practices that result in unequal opportunities and outcomes. Discrimination can manifest in various forms across different contexts, including employment, education, housing, healthcare, and public services.

Importantly, discrimination can be both subtle and covert, such as microaggressions, implicit bias, or exclusionary practices that are not overtly hostile but still contribute to systemic inequality. Conversely, it can also be hostile and overt, characterized by blatant acts of prejudice, harassment, or discriminatory policies that are openly expressed. Understanding these nuances is crucial for recognizing and addressing discrimination in its many forms.

Workplace discrimination is defined in legal terms as the unfair treatment of an employee or job applicant based on certain protected characteristics as established by federal, state, and local laws.

In a legal context, discrimination can manifest through various employment practices, including hiring, firing, promotions, compensation, job assignments, training, and other terms and conditions of employment.

Victims of discrimination have the right to file complaints with relevant agencies such as the Equal Employment Opportunity Commission (EEOC) and state and city civil rights agencies.

Key Elements of Discrimination:

1. **Unjust Treatment:** Discrimination occurs when individuals are treated differently or unfairly compared to others. This can include overt actions, such as refusing to hire someone based on their race, or more subtle forms, such as excluding individuals from opportunities based on preconceived notions or stereotypes.

2. **Protected Characteristics:** Many legal frameworks identify specific characteristics that are protected from discrimination. These often include:

- ○ **Race, Color, and National Origin:** Treating individuals differently based on their racial or ethnic background or color.

- ○ **Gender and Sex:** Discrimination based on an individual's gender identity or expression, including issues like wage gaps, sexual harassment, and unequal opportunities in the workplace.

- ○ **Sexual Orientation and Gender Identity:** Treating individuals differently based on their sexual orientation or gender identity, which can manifest in harassment or exclusion.

- ○ **Disability:** Discrimination against individuals with physical or mental disabilities, including failure to provide reasonable accommodations.

- ○ **Pregnancy:** Discrimination against individuals based on pregnancy, childbirth, or related medical conditions. This can include unfair treatment in hiring, promotions, job assignments, or termination, as well as failure to provide necessary accommodations during pregnancy.

- ○ **Familial Status:** Discrimination based on an individual's status as a parent or guardian. This can manifest in various ways, such as refusing to rent to families with children, imposing different terms or conditions on families, or excluding families from certain housing options. Familial status discrimination can significantly impact access to safe and suitable housing.

- ○ **Age:** Unequal treatment of individuals based on their age, particularly affecting older adults in employment and services.

- ○ **Religion:** Discrimination based on an individual's religious beliefs or practices, often seen in workplace policies or public accommodations.

- ○ **Genetic Information:** Discrimination based on an individual's genetic information or predispositions, including adverse treatment in employment or health insurance due to genetic testing results or family medical history.

3. **Forms of Discrimination: Discrimination can be classified into several forms, including:**

   o Direct Discrimination: Explicitly treating someone less favorably due to a protected characteristic.

   o Indirect Discrimination: Policies or practices that appear to be neutral but disproportionately affect individuals from certain groups.

   o Harassment: Unwelcome conduct based on a protected characteristic that creates a hostile environment.

   o Retaliation: Adverse actions taken against individuals for asserting their rights or filing complaints regarding discrimination.

4. **Impact on Individuals and Society:** The effects of discrimination can be profound and far-reaching. Victims may experience emotional distress, reduced opportunities, and negative impacts on their mental and physical health. On a societal level, discrimination perpetuates inequality, undermines social cohesion, and hampers economic growth by limiting the potential contributions of marginalized groups.

5. **Legal Frameworks:** Numerous laws and regulations exist to combat discrimination, including the Civil Rights Act, the Americans with Disabilities Act, and the Age Discrimination in Employment Act. These laws are designed to promote equality and provide mechanisms for individuals to seek redress.

Discrimination is a multifaceted issue that extends beyond individual actions to reflect broader societal attitudes and structures. Understanding its definition, forms, and implications is essential for recognizing and addressing discrimination effectively, fostering a more equitable and just society.

Legal Definitions vs. Societal Perceptions:

The legal definitions of discrimination are often established by laws and regulations, which can vary across jurisdictions. For example, what constitutes discrimination under federal law may differ from state or local laws.

Societal perceptions of discrimination can shift based on cultural context and awareness. For example, certain actions might be perceived as discriminatory by the public but may not be legally actionable under existing laws.

Discriminatory Employment Practices Examples

Recognizing the specific actions that constitute workplace discrimination is crucial for employees to identify and address issues effectively. Below are detailed examples of common discriminatory practices:

1. Hiring and Recruitment Practices:

- **Job Interviews with Discriminatory Questions**: During interviews, employers may ask inappropriate questions that relate to an applicant's protected status, such as marital status, childbearing plans, or age. For example, an interviewer might ask a female applicant, "Are you planning to have children soon?" or question an older applicant, "How do you keep up with new technology?" These questions could influence the hiring decision and reflect discriminatory bias.

- **Refusal to Consider Non-Traditional Candidates**: Employers may reject applicants with non-traditional backgrounds, such as those without a college degree or those who have taken career breaks for caregiving, assuming that these candidates are "less committed" or not suitable for the role. This may disproportionately affect women or older applicants.

2. Promotion and Advancement Opportunities:

- **Glass Ceiling Effect**: Despite demonstrating excellent job performance, women, particularly women of color, may find that there are invisible barriers that prevent them from reaching senior leadership roles. Even when they exceed expectations, they may be passed over for promotions in favor of male colleagues, with their qualifications and contributions overlooked due to gender or racial biases.

- **Overlooking Performance for Family Obligations**: An employee who has taken maternity or paternity leave, or requests flexible hours to care for a sick family member, may find that their performance is scrutinized more harshly than those who don't have family obligations. For instance, a new father may be given fewer opportunities for leadership roles because of perceived "commitment issues" related to his parenting responsibilities.

- **Unequal Evaluation Criteria**: Some employees may be unfairly judged by higher standards due to their identity. For example, a Black employee may find that their work is scrutinized more intensely than a white colleague's work, despite delivering similar or higher-quality results. These unequal evaluation standards can limit promotion opportunities.

3. Workplace Harassment:

- **Sexual Harassment**: Sexual harassment includes unwelcome comments, physical gestures, or advances based on gender. A male supervisor might make inappropriate comments about an employee's appearance or discuss their sexual preferences, creating an uncomfortable and unsafe environment for employees of any gender.

- **Retaliation for Reporting Harassment**: An employee who reports harassment based on race, gender, or disability might find themselves retaliated against by the employer. This can include being passed over for promotions, having work responsibilities reduced, or even being fired. Retaliation can prevent employees from speaking out and perpetuate a toxic work culture.

- **Microaggressions**: Subtle, often unintentional comments or actions that belittle a person's race, gender, sexual orientation, or other protected characteristic. For example, a manager might say to a Hispanic employee, "You speak really good English," implying that speaking English fluently is unexpected based on their ethnicity.

4. Compensation and Benefits:

- **Unequal Pay for Equal Work**: Women, people of color, and other marginalized groups are often paid less than their counterparts for performing the same job at the same level. For example, a woman working as an executive may discover that her male peers with similar qualifications and responsibilities are making more money. These wage gaps reflect systemic gender and racial biases in compensation practices.

- **Inconsistent Bonuses or Promotions**: Certain employees may be unfairly denied bonuses or promotions due to their race, gender, or family status. For instance, a pregnant employee may be excluded from the company's annual bonus pool or a senior employee may be overlooked for a promotion because they requested a flexible work schedule due to childcare obligations.

- **Discriminatory Healthcare Benefits**: Some employees, particularly LGBTQ+ workers or employees with disabilities, may find that their healthcare benefits do not adequately cover their needs. For example, an employee who is transgender may discover that their healthcare plan does not cover gender-affirming surgeries or related medical treatments.

5. Job Assignments and Work Conditions:

- **Discriminatory Task Distribution**: Employees may be assigned less important, less challenging, or menial tasks due to their gender, race, or disability. For example, a woman of color in an office setting may consistently be asked to handle administrative tasks rather than project management roles, despite being more qualified.

- **Unreasonable Work Conditions**: Employees with disabilities may face significant challenges in the workplace, such as being denied reasonable accommodations. For instance, an employee with mobility challenges might request an accessible workspace or an alternative chair, but their employer refuses, citing costs or inconvenience. Alternatively, a pregnant employee might be denied reasonable accommodations, such as the ability to sit rather than stand for long hours.

- **Gender or Racial Segregation of Roles**: Some workplaces may segregate tasks or departments by gender or race, with employees of a particular group being disproportionately assigned to less prestigious or lower-paying roles. For example, a Black woman may be steered into a customer service role rather than a leadership or creative position, despite her qualifications, based on assumptions about her abilities tied to racial stereotypes.

6. Disciplinary Actions:

- **Disproportionate Disciplinary Measures**: Employees from certain racial or ethnic groups may receive harsher penalties for similar infractions compared to their peers. For example, an Asian employee may receive a formal written warning for a minor mistake, while a white colleague who commits the same error does not face any disciplinary action.

- **Discriminatory Investigations**: In some cases, employees may find themselves unfairly targeted for disciplinary investigations based on their identity. For example, a Black employee might be scrutinized more heavily during an internal investigation than a white employee accused of similar behavior, reflecting racial biases in the company's disciplinary processes.

7. Employment Termination:

- **Discriminatory Firing Practices**: Employees who are pregnant, disabled, or belong to a marginalized group may face wrongful termination due to their protected status. For example, a transgender employee might be fired shortly after transitioning, with the employer citing performance issues, despite their excellent work record.

- **Stereotypical Assumptions in Layoffs**: During layoffs, employers may disproportionately target employees based on assumptions related to their gender, age, or family status. For example, older employees may be laid off under the assumption that they are less tech-savvy, or women may be disproportionately affected by layoffs due to gendered assumptions about their commitment to work.

8. Work-Life Balance Discrimination:

- **Discriminating Against Caregivers**: Employees who are primary caregivers (whether for children, elderly family members, or spouses) may face discrimination when requesting flexible work arrangements. For example, a male employee who requests flexible hours to care for his elderly father may be denied, while a female colleague receives the same benefit for caring for her children.

- **Unfair Denial of Parental Leave**: Female employees may experience discrimination when requesting parental leave. A female employee may find that her request for maternity leave is denied or that she is unfairly penalized for taking extended time off. Conversely, a male employee may not be allowed to take parental leave, or it may be questioned because of a cultural assumption that caregiving is primarily a woman's responsibility.

9. Retaliation:

- **Retaliation for Reporting Discrimination**: Employees who report discrimination, whether it's racial, gender-based, or disability-related, may face retaliation, such as being ostracized, denied opportunities, or even fired. For example, a Black employee who complains about racial harassment may find themselves unfairly written up for minor infractions or passed over for promotions.

- **Retaliation for Taking Family Leave**: Employees who take family or medical leave (such as maternity leave or leave for a disability) might experience retaliation upon their return to work, such as being assigned undesirable tasks or being excluded from important meetings and projects. This retaliatory treatment can make employees hesitant to assert their rights, particularly when they are already vulnerable.

These examples illustrate a range of discriminatory adverse actions that employees might face across different stages of employment, from hiring to termination, highlighting the many ways discrimination can manifest in the workplace. Understanding these examples can help employees identify potential discrimination and take appropriate action to protect their rights.

Understanding workplace discrimination involves recognizing both its legal and social definitions, as well as identifying specific actions that constitute discriminatory behavior. This foundational knowledge empowers employees to recognize discrimination in its many forms, fostering a proactive approach to addressing issues in their work environments. By illuminating these aspects, this chapter sets the stage for further exploration of strategies and protections available to combat discrimination in the workplace, enabling readers to advocate effectively for themselves and their colleagues.

1.2   The Legal Framework

Overview of Relevant Laws:

Numerous federal and state laws protect against discrimination, each addressing specific areas and characteristics. Here are some of the most significant:

Civil Rights Act of 1964:

This landmark legislation was a pivotal moment in the fight for civil rights in the United States. Title VII of the Act specifically prohibits discrimination based on race, color, religion, sex, or national origin in employment and public accommodations. The Act established the Equal Employment Opportunity

Commission (EEOC) to enforce its provisions, providing a mechanism for individuals to file complaints and seek redress.

Americans with Disabilities Act (ADA):

Enacted in 1990, the ADA is a comprehensive civil rights law that prohibits discrimination against individuals with disabilities in all areas of public life, including jobs, schools, transportation, and public accommodations. The ADA mandates that employers provide reasonable accommodations to qualified individuals with disabilities, ensuring they have equal access to employment opportunities.

Age Discrimination in Employment Act (ADEA):

Passed in 1967, the ADEA protects individuals aged forty and older from discrimination based on age in employment decisions, such as hiring, promotions, wages, and termination. The law aims to prevent age-based biases and stereotypes that can limit opportunities for older workers.

Equal Pay Act of 1963:

This law prohibits gender-based wage discrimination, requiring that men and women receive equal pay for equal work performed in the same establishment. The Act aims to eliminate the wage gap between genders and promote fair compensation practices.

Family and Medical Leave Act (FMLA):

The FMLA allows eligible employees to take up to 12 weeks of unpaid leave for certain family and medical reasons, including pregnancy and childbirth. This law provides job protection to ensure individuals can care for themselves and their families without fear of losing their jobs.

Pregnancy Discrimination Act (PDA) of 1978:

The PDA amends Title VII of the Civil Rights Act of 1964, prohibiting discrimination based on pregnancy, childbirth, or related medical conditions. It ensures that pregnant individuals are treated the same as other employees who are similar in their ability or inability to work.

Genetic Information Nondiscrimination Act (GINA) of 2008:

GINA prohibits discrimination in health coverage and employment based on genetic information. The law aims to prevent employers from using genetic information to make decisions about hiring, firing, or promotion, thus protecting individuals' privacy and encouraging them to seek genetic testing without fear of discrimination.

Fair Housing Act (FHA):

Enacted in 1968, the FHA prohibits discrimination in housing based on race, color, religion, sex, national origin, familial status, or disability. It aims to ensure equal housing opportunities for all individuals and to combat discriminatory practices in rental, sale, and financing of housing.

Section 504 of the Rehabilitation Act of 1973:

This law prohibits discrimination based on disability in programs and activities receiving federal financial assistance. It requires that individuals with disabilities have equal access to educational programs, employment, and other federally funded services.

LGBTQ+ Rights Legislation (e.g., Obergefell v. Hodges, 2015):

This Supreme Court ruling recognized the constitutional right to marry for same-sex couples, affirming that state bans on same-sex marriage are unconstitutional. It represents a significant legal victory for LGBTQ+ rights, promoting equality and protection under the law.

These laws represent foundational protections against discrimination in various contexts. Each law has its own enforcement mechanisms and requirements, making it crucial for individuals to understand their rights and the processes available to them.

Key Agencies Involved:

Equal Employment Opportunity Commission (EEOC)

The EEOC is a federal agency tasked with enforcing laws against workplace discrimination, primarily under Title VII of the Civil Rights Act of 1964, the Americans with Disabilities Act (ADA), and the Age Discrimination in Employment Act (ADEA), among others. Here are key aspects of the EEOC:

- **Filing Complaints**: Individuals who believe they have experienced workplace discrimination can file a charge with the EEOC. This process typically begins with a preliminary consultation, where the Complainant provides details about the alleged discrimination.

- **Investigation**: Once a charge is filed, the EEOC conducts a thorough investigation to determine whether there is reasonable cause to believe discrimination occurred. This may involve gathering evidence, interviewing witnesses, and reviewing documentation from both the Complainant and the employer.

- **Resolution**: If the EEOC finds reasonable cause, it attempts to mediate a resolution between the parties. If mediation fails, the EEOC may file a lawsuit on behalf of the Complainant or issue a "right to sue" letter, allowing the individual to pursue a private lawsuit.

- **Educational Role**: In addition to enforcement, the EEOC provides guidance and education to employers and employees about their rights and responsibilities under anti-discrimination laws, promoting awareness and compliance.

State Human Rights Commissions

State Human Rights Commissions operate at the state level to address discrimination in various areas, including employment, housing, and public accommodations. Each state may have its own specific commission with varying powers and responsibilities:

- **Complaint Handling**: Individuals can file complaints related to discrimination under state laws with their respective Human Rights Commission. These commissions often handle cases that may not fall under federal jurisdiction or that involve violations of state-specific laws.

- **Mediation and Investigation**: Similar to the EEOC, state commissions typically offer mediation services to help resolve disputes without the need for formal litigation. If mediation is unsuccessful, they will investigate the allegations, gathering evidence and testimonies.

- **Enforcement of State Laws**: Many states have their own anti-discrimination laws that may provide broader protections than federal laws. State commissions enforce these laws and can take legal action against violators.

- **Community Engagement**: State Human Rights Commissions often engage with the community to educate individuals about their rights, the complaint process, and the importance of diversity and inclusion.

Additional Agencies

While the EEOC and state Human Rights Commissions are the primary agencies involved in handling discrimination complaints, there are other relevant organizations and agencies:

- **Local Human Rights Commissions**: Some cities and counties have their own human rights or civil rights commissions that handle discrimination complaints at the local level. These commissions may focus on specific issues relevant to their communities or may expand upon federal and state discrimination laws.

- **Office for Civil Rights (OCR)**: Part of the U.S. Department of Education, the OCR addresses discrimination in educational institutions based on race, color, national origin, sex, disability, and age. It investigates complaints and enforces civil rights laws in education.

- **Department of Justice (DOJ)**: The DOJ can take action against discrimination in housing and public accommodations through its Civil Rights Division. It handles complaints related to violations of the Fair Housing Act and other civil rights laws.

Understanding the roles of these agencies is crucial for individuals seeking to file discrimination complaints, as each agency has its own procedures, protections, and areas of focus.

The Importance of Understanding the Legal Framework:

Familiarity with the legal framework helps individuals recognize when they are victims of discrimination and understand their rights and protections.

Knowing the appropriate channels for filing complaints is crucial for effectively addressing grievances and seeking justice.

1.3 Prevalence of Employment Discrimination and the Importance of Reporting

Discrimination remains a widespread issue in employment, affecting individuals' opportunities, career advancement, and workplace experiences. Understanding the types of employment discrimination most commonly reported is critical to addressing these issues and promoting a fairer and more inclusive work environment.

Statistics on Prevalent Types of Employment Discrimination

1. **Race Discrimination**

   o According to the Equal Employment Opportunity Commission (EEOC), in 2022, race-based discrimination made up 36% of all employment discrimination charges. Black and Hispanic workers, in particular, are disproportionately affected by hiring biases, unequal pay, and limited advancement opportunities in the workplace.

2. **Gender Discrimination**

   o Gender discrimination, which includes issues like sexual harassment and the gender pay gap, accounted for 29% of all employment discrimination complaints filed with the EEOC. Women, as well as gender minorities, continue to face significant challenges in securing equal opportunities, pay, and treatment in the workplace.

3. **Disability Discrimination**

   o Discrimination based on disability comprised 32% of all charges filed with the EEOC in 2022. This includes the failure of employers to provide reasonable accommodations for employees with disabilities and the widespread barriers to workplace accessibility, which affect individuals' ability to thrive in their roles.

4. **Age Discrimination**

   o Age-related discrimination remains prevalent, with workers over forty often facing bias in hiring, promotions, and layoffs. Though data varies, older employees frequently encounter stereotypes that hinder their job prospects and career growth.

Importance of Reporting Employment Discrimination

Reporting discrimination is crucial for several important reasons:

1. **Promoting Accountability**

   o Filing a discrimination complaint holds employers accountable for their actions. It helps ensure that workplaces adhere to anti-discrimination laws and policies, ensuring fair treatment for all employees.

2. **Data Collection and Analysis**

   o Reports of discrimination provide valuable data that civil rights agencies, like the EEOC, can analyze to identify patterns of discrimination. This data is essential for understanding where systemic issues exist and helps allocate resources to tackle the most pressing problems.

3. **Legal Recourse**

   o Reporting discrimination is often the first step toward seeking legal recourse. Once a claim is filed, individuals can pursue remedies such as compensation, policy changes, or better practices in the workplace. Reporting is essential to initiate investigations and legal action.

4. **Raising Public Awareness**

   o Documented instances of workplace discrimination help raise public awareness of the issue. This awareness can prompt broader societal change, as well as shift organizational and government policies toward greater equity and inclusion.

5. **Encouraging Policy Change**

   o Collective reporting can bring attention to patterns of discrimination that require legislative or regulatory reform. By highlighting widespread discriminatory practices, employees can help drive the creation of policies that promote fairness and justice in the workplace.

Discrimination in employment continues to be a pervasive issue, impacting employees' opportunities and work experiences in significant ways. By understanding the prevalence of different types of discrimination—such as race, gender, disability, and age discrimination—we can better identify and address the inequalities that persist in the workplace.

Reporting discrimination is essential for holding employers accountable, providing data for analysis, and pursuing legal remedies. It also serves as a powerful tool for raising awareness, encouraging systemic change, and fostering more inclusive workplace environments.

In the next chapter, we will explore the various forms of discrimination in greater detail and discuss the legally protected characteristics that are essential in recognizing discriminatory behavior. By learning to identify and address discrimination, employees can help create a more just and equitable workplace for all.

Chapter 2: Types of Discrimination

2.1 Race, National Origin, and Color Discrimination

Definition and Scope

- **Racial and National Origin Discrimination**:

  - Racial discrimination involves unfair treatment of individuals based on their race, while national origin discrimination targets individuals based on their cultural or national origin. Legally, these definitions encompass actions such as exclusion from employment, unequal pay, and lack of access to education or housing based on these characteristics.

- **Color Discrimination**:

  - A specific type of racial discrimination, color discrimination occurs when individuals are treated differently due to their skin color or tone. This form of discrimination can manifest within racial groups, leading to colorism, where individuals with lighter skin are often afforded preferential treatment over those with darker skin.

Historical Context

- **Systemic Racism**:

  - The history of systemic racism in the U.S. is rooted in slavery, segregation, and discriminatory laws that have historically marginalized non-white populations. This legacy has contributed to ongoing disparities in wealth, education, and health outcomes, reinforcing social hierarchies.

- **Impact of Colorism**:

  - Colorism has deep roots in colonialism and slavery, where lighter skin was often associated with higher social status. This preference has perpetuated internal divisions within racial communities, impacting self-image and social mobility.

Impact on Hiring and Promotion

- **Disparities in Hiring Practices:** Studies consistently demonstrate that candidates from racial and ethnic backgrounds, particularly Black, Latinx, Asian, and Indigenous individuals, face significant barriers during the hiring process. For instance, research indicates that applicants with names perceived as "ethnic" often receive fewer callbacks than those with traditionally Anglo names, even when their qualifications are identical. This phenomenon, known as "name-based discrimination," highlights systemic biases entrenched in hiring practices.

- **Promotion Challenges:** Once employed, individuals from racial and ethnic minorities may encounter additional hurdles in career advancement. These challenges can stem from systemic barriers, such as a lack of access to mentorship opportunities and professional networks, which are critical for navigating career trajectories. Research has shown that minority employees are often overlooked for promotions, perpetuating a lack of diversity in leadership positions and reinforcing a homogeneous workplace culture.

- **Workplace Culture and Inclusion:** The impact of race and ethnicity extends beyond hiring and promotions. Employees from diverse backgrounds may experience microaggressions—subtle, often unintentional discriminatory comments or behaviors—that can create a hostile work environment. Moreover, the absence of representation in leadership roles can lead to feelings of isolation and undervaluation among minority employees. Organizations that fail to prioritize diversity, equity, and inclusion risk diminished employee morale and increased turnover, as individuals seek workplaces that genuinely value and respect their contributions.

Legal Protections

Title VII of the Civil Rights Act:

This legislation prohibits employment discrimination based on race, color, religion, sex, or national origin. Title VII empowers individuals to file complaints against employers who engage in discriminatory practices, establishing a legal framework for addressing racial and color discrimination.

Civil Rights Act of 1964 (Title VII):

This landmark law prohibits discrimination based on race, color, religion, sex, or national origin in employment and public accommodations. Title VII specifically prohibits employers from making employment decisions based on these characteristics.

Voting Rights Act of 1965:

This act aims to eliminate barriers to voting for African Americans and other racial minorities. It prohibits discriminatory voting practices and requires jurisdictions with significant racial discrimination histories to obtain federal approval before changing voting laws.

Fair Housing Act of 1968:

This act prohibits discrimination based on race, color, religion, sex, national origin, familial status, or disability in housing. It aims to ensure equal housing opportunities for all individuals.

Equal Educational Opportunities Act of 1974:

This act prohibits discrimination against students based on race, color, sex, or national origin in public schools and educational programs. It requires that schools provide equal educational opportunities.

Section 1981 of the Civil Rights Act of 1866:

This statute prohibits racial discrimination in the making and enforcement of contracts, including employment contracts. It allows individuals to sue for damages if they experience discrimination based on race in contract-related matters.

Race Relations Act (1965, amended 1976):

Although primarily a British law, it is noteworthy for prohibiting racial discrimination in public places and employment. The principles influenced U.S. civil rights legislation.

Americans with Disabilities Act (ADA) (1990):

While primarily focused on disability discrimination, the ADA also provides protections for individuals with disabilities who may face intersectional discrimination based on race.

- **Key Case Studies**:

  - **Loving v. Virginia (1967)**: This case challenged laws prohibiting interracial marriage, emphasizing that racial classifications used to restrict personal relationships are discriminatory and unconstitutional.

  - **Johnson v. Santa Clara Transportation Agency (1987)**: This case involved affirmative action, where the Supreme Court ruled that race and color could be considered in hiring decisions to promote diversity, reflecting the need to rectify historical injustices.

Contemporary Issues

- **Racial Profiling**:

  - Racial profiling involves law enforcement targeting individuals based on race rather than behavior. This practice has significant implications for civil rights and can lead to wrongful arrests and a loss of trust in law enforcement.

- **Disparities in Education and Housing**:

  - Individuals with darker skin often face systemic barriers in education and housing, such as discriminatory lending practices and inequitable school funding. These disparities perpetuate cycles of poverty and limit opportunities for advancement.

- **Influence of Colorism**:

  - Colorism affects various aspects of life, including media representation, employment opportunities, and social dynamics. It can lead to internalized biases and affect the self-esteem of individuals with darker skin.

Examples of Race, Color, and National Origin Discrimination in Employment:

1. Scenario: Racial Discrimination in Hiring

The Incident:

Julia, a qualified Hispanic candidate, applies for a management position at a well-known tech company. Despite impressing the hiring panel with her experience and ideas, the company hires a less experienced white candidate. Later, Julia learns that the hiring manager expressed a preference for candidates who "fit the company culture," which is predominantly white.

Explanation:

This situation constitutes **racial discrimination** under Title VII of the **Civil Rights Act of 1964**. Title VII prohibits employers from discriminating against employees or job applicants based on race, color, national origin, sex, or religion. The hiring decision appears to have been influenced by Julia's race, which violates the provisions of Title VII that mandate equal treatment in hiring practices.

2. Scenario: Color Discrimination in Promotion

The Incident:

Patrick, a Black man, has worked at a marketing firm for three years and has received positive performance reviews. He applies for a management position, but the company promotes a lighter-skinned Black woman instead. Later, Patrick hears that one of the committee members preferred a candidate with a "more polished look," which was associated with lighter skin tones.

Explanation:

This situation suggests **color discrimination**, which is a form of racial discrimination, also prohibited under **Title VII of the Civil Rights Act of 1964**. Color discrimination occurs when an employer treats an employee unfairly due to their skin tone, even if they belong to the same racial group. In this case, the preference for a lighter-skinned individual over a more qualified darker-skinned individual violates Patrick's right to be considered for promotion without regard to color.

3. Scenario: Racial Harassment in the Workplace

The Incident:

Tyler, a Black employee, experiences coworkers making derogatory jokes about his race during team meetings. At first, Tyler ignores it, but the comments escalate, and he feels increasingly uncomfortable. After asking a colleague to stop, Tyler reports the behavior to HR. Despite his report, HR does not follow up, and the jokes continue, leaving Tyler isolated and stressed.

Explanation:

This constitutes **racial harassment** in violation of **Title VII of the Civil Rights Act of 1964**. Harassment based on race creates a hostile work environment and is illegal under federal law. The employer's failure to act on Tyler's complaints and allow the harassment to persist shows a lack of proper response, further violating Tyler's rights under Title VII, which mandates employers take reasonable steps to prevent and address workplace harassment.

4. Scenario: Racial Bias in the Hiring Process

The Incident:

Chance, a talented Black software developer, interviews for a job at a top tech company. He is told he was rejected because he "lacked confidence," but he later learns the position went to a white candidate with less relevant experience. Chance believes his race may have been a factor in the hiring decision.

Explanation:

Chance's experience suggests **racial discrimination** in violation of **Title VII of the Civil Rights Act of 1964**. The employer's decision to reject Chance based on factors unrelated to his qualifications—such as his race—violates the law, which requires employers to make employment decisions without regard to race. The company's preference for a white candidate over an equally or more qualified Black candidate may constitute discriminatory hiring practices.

5. Scenario: National Origin Discrimination in Hiring

The Incident:

Fatima, an immigrant from Syria, applies for a customer service role at a call center. Despite her relevant experience and fluency in English, she is passed over for a native-born American candidate who has less experience. Fatima later finds out the hiring manager preferred "local talent" and expressed concerns about her accent and background.

Explanation:

Fatima's situation appears to be **national origin discrimination**, which is prohibited under **Title VII of the Civil Rights Act of 1964**. Title VII protects employees from discrimination based on their national origin, including being passed over for a job due to their accent, birthplace, or ethnic background. The hiring manager's preference for "local talent" and focus on Fatima's national origin and accent may have influenced the decision, which violates her rights under this law.

6. Scenario: Reverse Harassment and Lack of Support

The Incident:

Clara, a white employee, experiences coworkers making jokes about white people during team meetings. Initially dismissing it as harmless, Clara eventually feels uncomfortable and isolated as the jokes escalate. She reports the harassment to HR, but her concerns are ignored, and the behavior continues, leaving Clara unsupported.

Explanation:

This scenario involves **reverse harassment**, where an employee from the majority group faces discriminatory behavior. While harassment based on race or ethnicity is typically thought of in the context of minority groups, **Title VII of the Civil Rights Act of 1964** prohibits harassment for all employees, regardless of race. Clara's employer has failed to address the harassment, creating a hostile work environment, which violates her right to a safe and respectful workplace under the Civil Rights Act.

These scenarios show how discrimination and harassment, in various forms, violate federal employment laws, specifically Title VII of the **Civil Rights Act of 1964**, which mandates fair treatment in hiring, promotion, and workplace conduct, free from bias based on race, color, national origin, and other protected categories. By understanding how the law applies in these scenarios, employees can better recognize when their rights have been violated and take appropriate steps to seek recourse.

2.2 Gender and Sex Discrimination

Gender and Sex Discrimination

- **Definition**:

  - Gender or Sex discrimination refers to unfair treatment based on an individual's gender or sex. It encompasses various forms of discrimination, including sexual harassment, unequal pay, and denial of opportunities based on gender stereotypes.

- **Forms of Discrimination**:

  - Common examples include workplace harassment, gender-based wage gaps, and biased hiring practices that favor one gender over another. Legal implications arise when these practices violate federal or state laws.

Impact on Women and Gender Identity

- **Sex Discrimination Overview:** Sex discrimination encompasses unfair treatment based on an individual's sex, including biases against women and non-binary individuals. This discrimination can manifest in various ways, including pay inequality, biased performance evaluations, and unequal access to promotions and leadership roles.

- **Challenges for Women:** Women often encounter stereotypes questioning their leadership capabilities, leading to fewer opportunities for advancement. Studies have shown that women are frequently assigned tasks deemed "less critical" or receive less support for professional development. Additionally, issues such as the glass ceiling—a metaphorical barrier preventing women from reaching top leadership positions—continue to persist in many industries.

- **Impact on Non-Binary and Gender Non-Conforming Individuals:** Non-binary individuals and those who do not conform to traditional gender roles may face additional challenges, including discrimination and harassment. Workplace policies that fail to acknowledge diverse gender identities can lead to feelings of exclusion and may discourage individuals from being their authentic selves.

Key Legislation

- **Title IX**:

    o Title IX of the Education Amendments of 1972 prohibits sex-based discrimination in any education program receiving federal funding. This law has been instrumental in promoting gender equality in sports, education, and extracurricular activities, ensuring equal opportunities for all genders.

- **Equal Pay Act of 1963**:

    o This act mandates equal pay for equal work, prohibiting wage disparities based on gender. Despite its enactment, wage gaps persist, highlighting ongoing challenges in achieving pay equity and the need for further legislative action.

Examples of Sex and Gender Discrimination:

1. Scenario: Gender Discrimination in Promotion

The Incident:

Leah, a qualified female engineer, applies for a senior engineering position at her company. Despite her excellent performance and significant contributions, the position is given to a male colleague with similar experience but less impressive results. Leah later learns that the hiring committee expressed concerns about her "fit" for the role, citing stereotypes about women being less assertive or capable of leading technical teams.

Explanation:

Leah's case constitutes **gender discrimination** in violation of **Title VII of the Civil Rights Act of 1964**. Title VII prohibits discrimination based on sex in hiring, promotions, and other employment decisions. The committee's decision to favor a male candidate based on gender stereotypes about leadership and assertiveness, rather than on qualifications or performance, violates Leah's right to be considered equally for the promotion. The decision was influenced by gender biases, which is unlawful under Title VII.

2. Scenario: Gender Discrimination in Hiring

The Incident:

Jordan, a skilled male marketing professional, applies for a project lead position at his advertising agency. Despite having more experience than the selected female candidate, Jordan is not chosen for the role. He learns from a coworker that the hiring manager had a bias toward female candidates for leadership roles and felt that men were less collaborative and more aggressive.

Explanation:

This is an example of **sex discrimination** in violation of **Title VII of the Civil Rights Act of 1964**. The hiring manager's bias against Jordan based on his gender and the assumption that men are less collaborative constitutes discriminatory treatment. Under Title VII, employers are prohibited from making employment decisions based on gender or gender stereotypes. Jordan's qualifications and experience should have been the primary factors in the hiring decision, not his gender.

3. Scenario: Sexual Harassment by a Supervisor

The Incident:

Samantha, a junior sales associate, faces ongoing inappropriate behavior from her supervisor, Mark. He comments on her appearance, sends suggestive messages, and pressures her to socialize after work hours, despite her refusals. When Mark's behavior escalates and creates a hostile work environment, Samantha reports it to HR. However, HR fails to take action, and Mark's behavior continues.

Explanation:

This situation constitutes **sexual harassment** under **Title VII of the Civil Rights Act of 1964**. Sexual harassment is illegal when it creates a hostile or intimidating work environment, as it has in Samantha's case. The behavior from her supervisor, including unsolicited comments about her appearance, suggestive messages, and unwanted advances, creates an environment in which Samantha feels uncomfortable and unsafe. HR's failure to take timely action to address her complaint constitutes employer negligence in responding to the harassment, further violating her rights under Title VII.

In each of these cases, the law has been violated due to discriminatory actions or harassment based on gender or sex. Title VII of the **Civil Rights Act of 1964** provides protections against such behaviors, ensuring that all employees are treated fairly and without bias in the workplace. The laws are designed to create a work environment free from discrimination, harassment, and stereotyping, allowing employees to perform their jobs without fear of retaliation or mistreatment based on their sex or gender.

2.3 Sexual Orientation and Gender Identity Discrimination

- **Definitions**:

  - **Sexual Orientation Discrimination** refers to the unfair treatment of individuals based on their actual or perceived sexual orientation. This can include discrimination against people who identify as heterosexual, homosexual, bisexual, or any other sexual orientation. Such discrimination may manifest in various contexts, including employment, housing, healthcare, and public accommodations, often resulting in unequal opportunities and treatment.

  - **Gender Identity Discrimination** involves the unjust treatment of individuals based on their gender identity or expression. This includes discrimination against those who identify as transgender, non-binary, or any gender identity that differs from the sex assigned at birth. This type of discrimination can occur in numerous areas, such as the workplace, educational settings, and healthcare, leading to barriers in accessing services and opportunities.

Issues for LGBTQ+ Employees

- **LGBTQ+ Issues Overview:** Employees identifying as LGBTQ+ may face unique challenges in the workplace, including overt harassment, exclusion from social events, or discriminatory policies. Societal biases and misunderstandings about sexual orientation and gender identity can create an unwelcoming environment that stifles authenticity and productivity.

- **Impact on Job Satisfaction and Retention:** The lack of inclusive workplace cultures can lead to a fear of being open about one's sexual orientation or gender identity, negatively impacting job satisfaction, mental health, and overall performance. Studies indicate that LGBTQ+ employees who feel accepted in their workplaces are more engaged and productive. Conversely, those who experience discrimination may seek employment elsewhere, leading to high turnover rates that can disrupt organizational stability.

- **Legal Protections and Resources:** While legal protections against sexual orientation discrimination vary by jurisdiction, many organizations are adopting inclusive policies and practices. Employee resource groups, diversity training, and inclusive benefits can foster a supportive environment that enhances retention and satisfaction for LGBTQ+ employees.

- **Key Cases:**

    o **Obergefell v. Hodges (2015):** This case legalized same-sex marriage nationwide, affirming the rights of same-sex couples and reinforcing the principle of equality under the law.

    o **Bostock v. Clayton County (2020):** The Supreme Court ruled that discrimination based on sexual orientation or gender identity constitutes a violation of Title VII, expanding protections for LGBTQ+ individuals in the workplace.

Current Challenges

- **Workplace Harassment:**

    o The #MeToo movement has highlighted widespread issues of harassment and discrimination against women and marginalized genders in various industries. This has led to increased calls for accountability and systemic change.

- **Intersectionality:**

    o LGBTQ+ individuals of color often face compounded discrimination due to overlapping identities. Recognizing the intersection of various social identities is crucial for understanding and addressing the unique challenges faced by these individuals.

Examples of Sexual Orientation Discrimination

1. Scenario: Sexual Harassment and Hostile Work Environment

The Incident:

Chris, a software developer, comes out as gay to his colleagues at a mid-sized tech company. While most of his coworkers are supportive, one team member, Jake, begins making derogatory comments and jokes about LGBTQ+ individuals during team meetings. Initially, Chris tries to brush it off, but Jake's behavior escalates over time. He specifically targets Chris, spreading rumors and making inappropriate jokes about Chris's relationship, creating a hostile work environment for him. When Chris reports the behavior to HR, his concerns are ignored, and Jake's harassment continues unabated.

Explanation:

Chris's experience constitutes **sexual harassment** in violation of **Title VII of the Civil Rights Act of 1964**, which prohibits discrimination based on sex, including harassment based on sexual orientation. Jake's comments and behavior create a hostile work environment, making it difficult for Chris to perform his job or feel safe at work. Furthermore, the company's failure to take action after Chris reports the harassment constitutes **employer negligence**. The law mandates that employers take prompt and effective steps to address harassment and protect employees from such discrimination. In this case, the company's inaction violates Chris's right to a harassment-free workplace under Title VII.

2. Scenario: Discrimination and Harassment Based on Gender Identity

The Incident:

Taylor, a transgender woman, works as a marketing coordinator at a large firm. After transitioning, she shares her gender identity with her colleagues to foster inclusivity, but one colleague, Sam, begins to make derogatory comments. He misgenders Taylor, using her former name and male pronouns despite being corrected. He also makes remarks during team meetings questioning the legitimacy of her transition and suggesting it's "just a phase." These comments cause Taylor significant distress, making it hard for her to focus at work. Despite approaching her manager and reporting the issue, Sam's behavior continues, and HR never follows up on the complaint.

Explanation:

This scenario involves **gender identity discrimination** and **harassment** in violation of **Title VII of the Civil Rights Act of 1964**, as amended by the **Equality Act** (2021), which extends protection to transgender employees. Sam's intentional misgendering and derogatory remarks about Taylor's transition create a hostile and discriminatory work environment. The failure of the company and HR to address Taylor's concerns, despite her reporting the issue, further violates her rights under the law. Discrimination and harassment based on gender identity or expression are unlawful, and the company is obligated to take swift and effective action to prevent and correct this behavior.

Key Legal Frameworks:

- **Title VII of the Civil Rights Act of 1964**: Title VII prohibits employment discrimination based on race, color, religion, sex, and national origin. It has been interpreted by courts and enforced by the **Equal Employment Opportunity Commission (EEOC)** to cover sexual orientation and gender identity discrimination in the workplace.

- **The Equality Act (2021)**: This act explicitly expands the protections of Title VII to include discrimination based on sexual orientation and gender identity. It ensures that transgender individuals and LGBTQ+ employees are entitled to the same protections against discrimination and harassment in employment as other workers.

- **Sexual Harassment**: Under Title VII, sexual harassment can include unwanted conduct based on a person's sex, gender, or sexual orientation. Harassment becomes unlawful when it creates a hostile work environment or when enduring the conduct becomes a condition of continued employment.

In both cases, the employees—Chris and Taylor—are entitled to protection under these laws, and their employers have failed to uphold their obligations to create a safe and respectful workplace. By allowing harassment and discrimination to continue unchecked, the company is violating their employees' civil rights under federal law.

2.4 Disability Discrimination

Understanding Disability

- **Definition**:

  - Disability encompasses a broad range of conditions, including physical, mental, and developmental disabilities. Legal definitions often focus on the functional limitations these conditions impose on individuals' daily lives.

- **Societal Perceptions**:

  - Societal attitudes toward disability significantly influence discrimination. Stigmatization and stereotypes can lead to exclusion and barriers in employment, education, and public services, perpetuating systemic inequalities.

Reasonable Accommodations and Barriers

- **Understanding Disability Discrimination:** Employees with disabilities may encounter discrimination through a lack of access to reasonable accommodations necessary for performing their jobs effectively. This can include modifications to workspaces, flexible scheduling, or adaptive technology that enables participation in various job functions.

- **Barriers to Inclusion:** Employers may fail to recognize their legal obligation to provide these accommodations, leading to a hostile or unwelcoming environment for individuals with disabilities. Misconceptions about the capabilities of disabled employees can also result in reluctance to hire or promote them, perpetuating cycles of marginalization and inequality.

- **Creating an Inclusive Environment:** Organizations can foster inclusivity by implementing comprehensive disability awareness training and creating clear policies regarding accommodations. By promoting a culture that values diversity, including disability, organizations can enhance morale and employee engagement.

Legal Framework

- **Americans with Disabilities Act (ADA):**

  - The ADA is a critical piece of legislation that prohibits discrimination against individuals with disabilities in various areas, including employment, public accommodations, and transportation. It aims to promote accessibility and inclusion in society.

- **Rehabilitation Act of 1973**:

  - This act laid the groundwork for disability rights, protecting individuals with disabilities from discrimination in federal programs and employment. It established the principle that people with disabilities should have equal access to opportunities.

Case Studies

- **Olmstead v. L.C.**:

  - This landmark case affirmed the right of individuals with disabilities to live in community settings rather than being institutionalized. It emphasized the importance of integration and the need for appropriate community services.

- **Accessibility in Public Spaces**:

  - Legal cases surrounding the ADA have highlighted the necessity of accessible facilities and services. Ensuring that public spaces accommodate individuals with disabilities is crucial for promoting equal rights.

Emerging Issues

- **Digital Accessibility**:

  - As technology continues to advance, the need for accessible digital platforms has become increasingly important. Many individuals with disabilities face challenges accessing online resources, prompting legal and policy discussions around digital rights.

- **Mental Health Stigma**:

  - Discrimination based on mental health conditions remains prevalent, often exacerbated by societal stigma. Ensuring workplace accommodations and fostering supportive environments is essential for promoting mental health equity.

Examples of Disability Discrimination

1. Scenario: Disability Discrimination in Job Assignment

The Incident:

Michael, a talented graphic designer, works at a marketing agency and has a visible physical disability that requires the use of a wheelchair. While the company has made some accommodations for his disability, Michael faces challenges when the company announces a major project that requires team collaboration and long hours. Michael expresses interest in taking on a leadership role, but his supervisor, Lisa, dismisses the idea, citing concerns about his ability to handle the physical demands despite Michael having successfully handled similar projects in the past. Lisa assigns the project to a less experienced colleague who does not have a disability. Michael feels frustrated and believes that the decision was based on stereotypes about his disability, not his actual qualifications.

Explanation:

Michael's supervisor's decision to deny him the leadership role based on assumptions about his disability constitutes **disability discrimination**, which violates the **Americans with Disabilities Act (ADA)**. The ADA prohibits discrimination against qualified individuals with disabilities in all areas of public life, including employment. Under the ADA, employers are required to provide reasonable accommodations and must not make employment decisions based on stereotypes or assumptions about an individual's abilities due to their disability. Michael has demonstrated the necessary qualifications, and the decision to exclude him from the role based on physical assumptions violates his rights under the ADA.

2. Scenario: Failure to Provide Reasonable Accommodations for Disability

The Incident:

Jasmine, an experienced project manager with a learning disability that affects her processing speed, has been open about her disability and receives accommodations, such as extra time to complete certain tasks. When a new manager, Tom, takes over, he is unaware of Jasmine's accommodation needs and pressures her to speed up her work, overlooking her established accommodations. When Jasmine attempts to explain her needs, Tom dismisses her and suggests she may not be suited for the role if she cannot keep up.

Jasmine feels frustrated and decides to file a complaint with HR. However, HR is indifferent and fails to address her concerns, and Tom's behavior continues unchecked.

Explanation:

Tom's actions, as well as HR's failure to take appropriate action, constitute a violation of the **Americans with Disabilities Act (ADA)**. Under the ADA, employers are required to provide **reasonable accommodations** to employees with disabilities to ensure they can perform their essential job functions. This includes adjusting work schedules, providing additional time, or modifying work processes to enable employees with disabilities to succeed. Tom's refusal to acknowledge Jasmine's established accommodations and the failure of HR to address the issue is a clear violation of the law, as it denies Jasmine the support she is legally entitled to in the workplace.

3. Scenario: Disability Harassment in the Workplace

The Incident:

Cara, a marketing coordinator who uses a wheelchair due to a spinal injury, works at a large advertising agency. While most colleagues are respectful, one team member, Tom, makes frequent inappropriate comments about her disability. He jokes about her needing "extra help" and makes sarcastic remarks when team meetings are held in locations that are not wheelchair accessible. Other team members notice and express discomfort, but Tom continues to target Cara, making her feel isolated and disrespected. When Cara reports the harassment to HR, they dismiss her concerns, telling her to "be more resilient" and claiming that they have more pressing issues to address.

Explanation:

Tom's comments and behavior toward Cara create a **hostile work environment**, which violates the **Americans with Disabilities Act (ADA)** and **Title VII of the Civil Rights Act of 1964**. Harassment based on a disability is unlawful under the ADA when it creates an environment that is intimidating, hostile, or offensive. Additionally, under the ADA, the employer is required to investigate and address complaints of disability-related harassment. The failure of HR to respond appropriately and the continued harassment Cara experiences is a violation of her rights, as employers have an obligation to maintain a workplace free from harassment based on a person's disability.

Key Legal Frameworks:

- **Americans with Disabilities Act (ADA):** This law prohibits discrimination against qualified individuals with disabilities in all aspects of employment, including hiring, promotion, job assignments, training, and compensation. It requires employers to provide reasonable accommodations to employees with disabilities, as long as the accommodations do not cause undue hardship to the business. It also makes it illegal to harass employees based on their disability.

- **Title VII of the Civil Rights Act of 1964:** While primarily concerned with discrimination based on race, color, religion, sex, and national origin, Title VII has been interpreted to apply to workplace harassment and to cover the discrimination of individuals with disabilities if the harassment is related to their disability.

Summary:

In all three scenarios, the individuals face discrimination, harassment, or a failure to receive reasonable accommodations related to their disability. These actions violate their rights under the **Americans with Disabilities Act (ADA)**, which protects employees from discrimination based on physical or mental disabilities. Employers are legally obligated to provide reasonable accommodations, create a workplace free from harassment, and take prompt and effective action when discrimination or harassment is reported. The failure of supervisors, HR, and management to address these issues leaves the employees vulnerable to ongoing mistreatment, which exacerbates their sense of isolation and frustration.

2.5 Pregnancy Discrimination

Definition:

- Pregnancy discrimination refers to the unfair treatment of individuals based on pregnancy, childbirth, or related medical conditions. This form of discrimination can occur in various contexts, including employment, healthcare, and education, leading to unequal opportunities and treatment for those who are pregnant or have recently given birth.

Forms of Discrimination:

- Common examples include denial of job opportunities, unfavorable treatment during hiring processes, refusal to provide reasonable accommodations, and adverse actions such as demotion or termination due to pregnancy. Legal implications arise when these practices violate federal or state laws designed to protect pregnant individuals.

Rights of Pregnant Employees

- **Pregnancy Discrimination Overview:** Discrimination against employees based on pregnancy, childbirth, or related medical conditions is prohibited under laws like the Pregnancy Discrimination Act. Pregnant employees are entitled to the same rights as any other employee regarding promotions, job security, and benefits.

- **Workplace Accommodations:** Employers are required to provide reasonable accommodations for pregnant employees, which may include adjusting work duties, providing flexible scheduling, or allowing for necessary breaks. Failure to accommodate these needs can lead to negative health outcomes for the employee and their child, as well as potential legal consequences for the employer.

- **Creating a Supportive Environment:** Establishing a supportive environment for pregnant employees involves clear communication about rights and accommodations. Organizations should foster open dialogue and provide resources to ensure that pregnant employees feel valued and supported during their pregnancy.

Key Legislation:

- **Pregnancy Discrimination Act (PDA) of 1978:**

The PDA amends Title VII of the Civil Rights Act of 1964, prohibiting discrimination based on pregnancy, childbirth, or related medical conditions. It ensures that pregnant individuals are treated the same as other employees who are similar in their ability or inability to work.

- **Family and Medical Leave Act (FMLA):**

The FMLA allows eligible employees to take up to 12 weeks of unpaid leave for certain family and medical reasons, including pregnancy and childbirth. This law aims to provide job protection and ensure that individuals can care for themselves and their families without fear of losing their jobs.

- **Pregnant Workers Fairness Act:**

This act requires employers to provide reasonable accommodations for workers affected by pregnancy, childbirth, or related medical conditions. It aims to ensure that pregnant employees can continue to work safely without facing discrimination.

- **PUMP Act (Providing Urgent Maternal Protections Act):**

The PUMP Act expands workplace protections for nursing parents, ensuring that they have the right to express breast milk during work hours. It requires employers to provide reasonable break time and a designated place for this purpose, promoting the health and well-being of both the parent and the child.

Current Challenges:

- **Workplace Accommodations:**

  - Many pregnant individuals face challenges in obtaining necessary accommodations, such as modified duties or flexible schedules, leading to stress and potential health risks. Employers may not fully understand their obligations under the law, resulting in inadequate support for pregnant employees.

- **Stigmatization:**

  - Stigma surrounding pregnancy in the workplace can lead to negative perceptions and treatment, impacting career advancement and job security. Addressing these biases is essential for fostering an inclusive work environment that supports pregnant employees.

Intersectionality:

- Pregnant individuals who belong to other marginalized groups, such as racial minorities or those with disabilities, may face compounded discrimination. Recognizing the intersection of various identities is crucial for understanding the unique challenges these individuals encounter in both workplace and healthcare settings.

Examples of Pregnancy Discrimination

1. Scenario: Pregnancy Discrimination in Job Assignment

The Incident:

Maya, a senior analyst at a financial services firm, announces her pregnancy to her manager, Karen. Shortly after, Karen begins to exhibit a noticeable shift in behavior toward Maya. Maya, who was initially being considered for a leadership role in an upcoming project, finds that the opportunity is suddenly reassigned to another employee without explanation. When Maya approaches Karen for feedback, Karen dismissively suggests that Maya should focus on her pregnancy instead of her work. As her due date approaches, Maya requests flexible work hours to accommodate prenatal appointments, but Karen denies the request, implying that Maya should "tough it out" like everyone else.

Explanation:

Karen's actions and refusal to accommodate Maya's needs constitute **pregnancy discrimination**, which violates the **Pregnancy Discrimination Act (PDA)**, an amendment to Title VII of the Civil Rights Act of 1964. The PDA prohibits discrimination on the basis of pregnancy, childbirth, or related medical conditions. Employers are required to treat pregnant employees the same as other employees who are temporarily disabled or have similar medical needs. By reallocating a leadership opportunity based on Maya's pregnancy and denying her request for flexible hours, Karen has discriminated against Maya due to her pregnancy. HR's failure to address the situation also reflects a violation of the law.

2. Scenario: Pregnancy Discrimination in Workload and Assignments

The Incident:

Jessica, a marketing coordinator at a retail company, is six months pregnant and has received positive performance reviews throughout her tenure. As her pregnancy progresses, she experiences complications that require more frequent medical appointments. She informs her supervisor, Mark, and requests a minor adjustment to her work schedule. Instead of offering support, Mark reacts negatively, expressing concern that her appointments might disrupt workflow. Shortly after, Mark starts assigning Jessica less critical tasks and excludes her from important team meetings. When Jessica raises her concerns, Mark implies that her pregnancy makes her less reliable, suggesting she can't handle her responsibilities.

Explanation:

Mark's treatment of Jessica constitutes **pregnancy discrimination**, which violates the **Pregnancy Discrimination Act (PDA)**. The PDA mandates that employers treat pregnant employees the same as other employees with medical conditions in terms of accommodations, assignments, and responsibilities. By assigning Jessica less critical tasks and excluding her from team meetings because of her pregnancy, Mark has discriminated against her. Additionally, HR's failure to respond to Jessica's complaint further exacerbates the situation and violates her rights under the law. Pregnancy-related medical needs must be treated equitably, and Jessica should not be penalized for requesting reasonable accommodations.

3. Scenario: Pregnancy Harassment in the Workplace

The Incident:

Sophie, a project manager at a tech firm, announces her pregnancy, and while most colleagues celebrate the news, one coworker, Lisa, begins to make negative comments about Sophie's ability to manage her workload. Lisa frequently questions Sophie's commitment, suggesting that Sophie should start planning for maternity leave, even though Sophie has not discussed such plans. As Sophie's pregnancy progresses, Lisa's comments escalate. In team meetings, Lisa makes sarcastic remarks like, "Are you sure you can handle this project? You won't want to be stressed out before the baby comes!" These remarks cause Sophie to feel belittled, anxious, and distracted, ultimately affecting her productivity and confidence.

Explanation:

Lisa's comments constitute **pregnancy-related harassment**, which is a form of **discrimination** under the **Pregnancy Discrimination Act (PDA)** and **Title VII of the Civil Rights Act of 1964**. Harassment based on pregnancy, childbirth, or related medical conditions creates a hostile work environment, which is unlawful under the PDA. Sophie is being subjected to unwanted comments and behaviors that negatively affect her well-being and ability to perform her job, which violates her rights under the law. HR's dismissive response to Sophie's complaint is also problematic, as they are obligated to take steps to address harassment in the workplace.

Key Legal Frameworks:

- **Pregnancy Discrimination Act (PDA):**

  The PDA is an amendment to Title VII of the Civil Rights Act of 1964. It prohibits discrimination on the basis of pregnancy, childbirth, or related medical conditions. The PDA requires that employers treat pregnancy the same as any other temporary disability or medical condition and that pregnant employees be allowed the same accommodations and treatment as employees with similar work restrictions.

- **Title VII of the Civil Rights Act of 1964:**

  Title VII prohibits employment discrimination based on sex, including pregnancy, childbirth, and related medical conditions. Title VII also prohibits sexual harassment, which includes harassment based on pregnancy. The law mandates that employers take reasonable steps to prevent and respond to harassment in the workplace.

Summary:

In each of these scenarios, the employees—Maya, Jessica, and Sophie—face different forms of **pregnancy discrimination** or **harassment** that violate their rights under the **Pregnancy Discrimination Act (PDA)** and **Title VII of the Civil Rights Act of 1964**. Discriminatory actions such as reallocating job assignments, refusing to provide accommodations, or making derogatory comments about a pregnant employee's abilities are unlawful. In addition, employers are required to take prompt and effective action when pregnancy-related harassment is reported. Failure to address these issues can result in continued discrimination, a hostile work environment, and legal consequences for the employer.

2.6 Familial Status Discrimination

Definition:

- Familial status discrimination refers to the unfair treatment of individuals based on their status as parents or guardians, particularly in housing and employment contexts. This form of discrimination encompasses not only those who have children but also individuals who are pregnant, those in the process of adopting, or those caring for family members. Familial status discrimination often results in unequal opportunities and can undermine the stability and well-being of families, limiting their access to safe and suitable housing and fair employment practices.

Employment Discrimination: In the workplace, familial status discrimination can manifest in several ways:

- ○ **Negative Treatment:** Employees with children may be passed over for promotions or raises due to assumptions that they are less committed to their jobs.

- ○ **Harassment or Retaliation:** Parents might experience harassment for needing flexible work hours to care for children or could face retaliation for taking parental leave.

- ○ **Lack of Support:** Employers may fail to provide employees with reasonable accommodations, such as flexible schedules or parental leave, which are essential for balancing work and family responsibilities.

Key Legislation:

- **Fair Housing Act (1968):**

  - ○ This landmark legislation prohibits discrimination in housing based on familial status, ensuring that families with children have equal access to housing opportunities. It aims to prevent practices that would segregate families and deny them the ability to live in certain neighborhoods.

- **Family and Medical Leave Act (FMLA):**

- o This act offers job protection for eligible employees who need to take unpaid leave for family-related reasons, such as the birth or adoption of a child. This law ensures that parents can navigate important life events and fulfill family responsibilities without the risk of losing their job.

Current Challenges:

- **Housing Access:**

  - o Families often face significant obstacles when searching for housing. Landlords may show bias against families with children, steering them toward less desirable neighborhoods or even refusing to rent altogether. Additionally, larger families may experience discrimination, with landlords unfairly labeling them as problematic or undesirable tenants due to the size of the family.

- **Workplace Flexibility:**

  - o Parents often struggle to obtain necessary accommodations to balance their professional and family responsibilities. Workplaces that lack supportive policies may inadvertently push parents to choose between their jobs and family needs, leading to stress, burnout, and even career setbacks. This lack of flexibility can disproportionately affect single parents or those with lower incomes who may not have the option to take unpaid leave.

Intersectionality:

- Individuals from marginalized groups, such as single parents, families of color, or LGBTQ+ parents, may face compounded discrimination. For example, a single mother of color may encounter bias not only for her familial status but also due to her race and gender, exacerbating the challenges she faces in housing and employment. Recognizing the intersection of various identities is crucial for understanding the unique obstacles these individuals encounter, necessitating tailored advocacy and policy responses to promote equality and inclusivity.

Conclusion:

- Familial status discrimination remains a significant barrier to achieving equality in housing and employment. Efforts to raise awareness, enforce existing laws, and create supportive environments for families are essential for fostering a society where all individuals, regardless of familial status, can thrive without discrimination or bias.

Examples of Familial Status Discrimination

1. Scenario: Familial Status Discrimination in Job Promotion

The Incident:

Vanessa, a customer service supervisor at a large retail chain, is a single mother of three children. After consistently receiving positive performance reviews, she applies for an open management position. During her interview with regional manager David, he raises concerns about her availability for the role, citing her status as a single mother. He questions whether she can handle the long hours and demands of the job, suggesting that her children might distract her from her work. Despite Vanessa's reassurances that she has reliable childcare and is committed to her career, David expresses skepticism and ultimately selects another candidate, stating the other person will be "more available" due to having fewer family obligations.

Explanation:

David's decision to consider Vanessa's familial status—specifically her responsibilities as a single mother—when selecting a candidate constitutes **familial status discrimination**, which is prohibited under the **Fair Housing Act (FHA)** and potentially under certain aspects of **Title VII of the Civil Rights Act** (depending on whether the employer is subject to discrimination laws related to familial status). **Familial status discrimination** occurs when an employer treats an employee unfavorably due to their status as a parent, or in this case, a single mother. The law prohibits discrimination based on the assumption that familial responsibilities hinder job performance, as was the case when David questioned Vanessa's availability due to her children. HR's dismissal of her concerns without further investigation further perpetuates the discrimination.

2. Scenario: Familial Status Harassment in the Workplace

The Incident:

Lucy, a single mother working as a sales associate at a retail store, frequently has to leave on time to pick up her child from daycare. While most of her colleagues are understanding, one coworker, Mike, makes derogatory comments about her family situation. He frequently jokes in front of other employees that Lucy should "get her priorities straight" and suggests that her child is a burden to her job performance. Over time, Mike escalates his remarks, implying that Lucy is "less dedicated" because she needs to leave on time and suggesting that her work will suffer because she "has too much on her plate." His comments create a hostile work environment for Lucy.

Explanation:

Mike's comments constitute **familial status harassment** under **Title VII of the Civil Rights Act of 1964** and, in some instances, under state or local laws that protect against discrimination based on familial status in the workplace. Harassment based on familial status is a form of discrimination where an employee is subjected to unwelcome comments or behavior due to their status as a parent or caretaker. Mike's repeated comments about Lucy's family responsibilities and her ability to balance them with her job create a hostile environment that interferes with her ability to work comfortably. The **Equal Employment Opportunity Commission (EEOC)** recognizes familial status as a protected class under Title VII when it results in harassment. HR's failure to address the issue or conduct a thorough investigation also violates workplace anti-discrimination policies.

Key Legal Frameworks:

- **Fair Housing Act (FHA)**: The FHA prohibits discrimination in housing based on several protected classes, including **familial status**. This means that landlords, real estate agents, and property managers cannot treat prospective tenants unfairly because they have children. Housing policies that impose restrictions on the number of children or suggest that families with children are unwelcome violate the FHA.

- **Title VII of the Civil Rights Act of 1964**: Title VII prohibits employment discrimination based on race, color, religion, sex, and national origin. It also prohibits **harassment** based on those protected characteristics, which can include familial status in certain circumstances. If an employee is harassed because of their family responsibilities or because they are a parent, and the harassment creates a hostile work environment, the employer can be held liable under Title VII.

- **State and Local Anti-Discrimination Laws**: Many states and localities have additional protections beyond federal law, including those that prohibit discrimination based on familial status in housing and employment. These laws can offer more robust protections depending on the jurisdiction.

Summary:

In these scenarios, **Vanessa and Lucy** both experience **familial status discrimination** or harassment, which violates **Title VII of the Civil Rights Act**. In Vanessa's case, the employer discriminates against her due to her status as a single mother when making a hiring decision. Lucy is subjected to harassment at work based on her responsibilities as a single mother, creating a hostile environment and violating Title VII protections. In both cases, the employers' failure to address these issues further reinforces the unlawful behavior and creates an ongoing, discriminatory environment for the individuals involved.

2.7 Age Discrimination

Overview of Age Discrimination

- **Definition**:
  - Age discrimination involves unfair treatment of individuals based on their age, particularly against those aged forty and older. It can manifest in various forms, including hiring practices, promotions, and layoffs.

- **Forms of Discrimination**:
  - Common examples include discriminatory hiring practices favoring younger candidates, failure to promote older employees, and workplace cultures that devalue older workers' contributions.

Stereotypes About Older Workers

- **Age Stereotypes:** Older employees often face stereotypes suggesting they are less adaptable, less technologically savvy, or resistant to change. Such misconceptions can adversely affect hiring decisions, promotional opportunities, and even job assignments, as employers may favor younger candidates based on unfounded assumptions.

- **Workplace Culture and Inclusivity:** Age discrimination may manifest in subtle ways, such as being excluded from training opportunities or innovative projects. This fosters a workplace culture where younger employees are favored for dynamic roles, potentially sidelining older workers who bring invaluable experience and diverse perspectives. Encouraging intergenerational collaboration can counteract age-related biases and enhance workplace culture.

- **The Value of Experience:** Organizations that recognize and leverage the experience of older employees often benefit from improved mentorship opportunities and a wealth of institutional knowledge. Promoting a culture of respect for all age groups can lead to enhanced teamwork and creativity, as diverse perspectives contribute to problem-solving.

Key Legislation

- **Age Discrimination in Employment Act (ADEA):**

  - The ADEA protects individuals aged forty and older from employment discrimination based on age. This legislation aims to promote the hiring and retention of older workers while challenging stereotypes about aging.

- **Significance of the Law:**

  - The ADEA has been instrumental in combating age-related biases, ensuring that older workers have equal opportunities to succeed in the workplace and challenging negative stereotypes associated with aging.

Important Cases

- **Smith v. City of Jackson:**

  - This case addressed age discrimination in hiring and promotion practices, establishing legal precedents regarding age-related claims and highlighting the need for clear standards in evaluating age discrimination cases.

Challenges Faced

- **Ageism in the Workplace**:

  - Negative stereotypes about older workers can lead to systematic bias in hiring and advancement. Addressing these perceptions is critical for fostering inclusive workplaces that value diverse age representation.

- **Balancing Workforce Diversity**:

  - Organizations increasingly recognize the importance of diverse age representation. However, achieving this balance requires overcoming entrenched biases and creating environments that support workers of all ages.

Examples of Age Discrimination

1. Scenario: Age Discrimination in Job Opportunity and Team Dynamics

The Incident:

George, a 58-year-old senior software engineer, has over 30 years of experience and consistently receives excellent performance reviews. However, after a company restructuring, a younger candidate, Jessica, is hired as the new team lead. Over time, George notices that Jessica frequently disregards his contributions, dismisses his ideas, and prioritizes suggestions from younger colleagues. She makes comments about needing "fresh perspectives" and implies that George's experience may be outdated. Despite his excellent track record, George is passed over for promotions, while younger team members are given leadership opportunities. He overhears Jessica stating that the company needs to "bring in younger talent" to stay relevant. Feeling marginalized, George approaches HR with concerns about age discrimination, presenting specific examples of how his age is influencing his treatment at work. However, HR dismisses his complaint, suggesting he is simply struggling to adjust to the new team dynamics.

Explanation:

Jessica's behavior and the company's failure to address George's concerns may violate the **Age Discrimination in Employment Act (ADEA)**, which prohibits discrimination against workers age 40 and older based on their age. The law protects employees from being treated unfairly because of age when it comes to hiring, firing, promotions, and other employment opportunities. In this case, George was overlooked for the team lead position and passed over for promotions in favor of younger colleagues, which may be indicative of **age discrimination**. Additionally, comments like "fresh perspectives" and the desire to bring in "younger talent" may constitute evidence that age played a role in these decisions. HR's failure to take George's complaint seriously and their dismissive response further demonstrates the company's lack of commitment to addressing age discrimination in the workplace.

2. Scenario: Exclusion and Marginalization Due to Age in the Workplace

The Incident:

Rose, a 62-year-old marketing director, has been with the company for over 25 years and has contributed significantly to its success. Recently, the company has focused on modernizing its branding and digital marketing strategies. During a team meeting, the CEO, Mark, emphasizes the need for a "younger, more dynamic team" to connect with millennial and Gen Z audiences, subtly implying that older employees may lack the insight or creativity needed for these initiatives. Afterward, Rose notices that she is excluded from key meetings and projects related to these new strategies. Younger team members are chosen to lead initiatives, and her suggestions are often ignored. She overhears Mark telling a colleague that the company needs to "get rid of the old guard" to foster innovation. Feeling marginalized, Rose approaches HR to express concerns about age discrimination, providing specific examples of exclusion and the negative impact of her age on her treatment. HR dismisses her complaint, suggesting that Rose may be struggling to adapt to the company's new direction and advising her to improve her collaboration with younger colleagues.

Explanation:

Mark's comments and the subsequent exclusion of Rose from key projects may constitute **age discrimination** under the **Age Discrimination in Employment Act (ADEA)**. The ADEA makes it illegal for employers to treat workers aged forty or older less favorably based on their age, particularly when it comes to job assignments, promotions, and job training. Mark's comment about needing a "younger, more dynamic team" and his remarks about "getting rid of the old guard" are discriminatory and suggest that Rose's age was a factor in excluding her from new opportunities. HR's dismissal of Rose's concerns without taking appropriate action further reflects the company's failure to prevent or address age-based discrimination.

3. Scenario: Age-Related Harassment in the Workplace

The Incident:

Anne, a 55-year-old project manager, has been with the company for over a decade. A younger team member, Jake, starts making disparaging comments about Anne's age. He frequently refers to her as "the old-timer" and jokes that she should "get with the times" when discussing new technologies or trends. Initially, Anne brushes off these remarks, but Jake's comments escalate over time. During team meetings, he makes jokes suggesting that older employees are resistant to change and less innovative. These remarks create an uncomfortable atmosphere for Anne, leaving her feeling disrespected and marginalized. She decides to report the harassment to HR, providing specific examples of Jake's comments and the negative impact on her morale and productivity. HR dismisses her concerns, suggesting the comments were not meant to be harmful and advising Anne to be more resilient. They imply that Anne should adapt to the team's dynamics rather than take offense.

Explanation:

Jake's comments may constitute **age-related harassment**, which is prohibited under the **Age Discrimination in Employment Act (ADEA)**. Harassment based on age is considered a form of discrimination when it creates a hostile work environment. In this case, Jake's repeated comments about Anne's age, referring to her as an "old-timer" and implying that older employees are resistant to change, could create such an environment. These comments may have interfered with Anne's ability to perform her job and caused emotional distress. HR's failure to take appropriate action to investigate or address this behavior reflects a violation of the employer's responsibility to maintain a work environment free from age-based harassment.

Key Legal Frameworks:

- **Age Discrimination in Employment Act (ADEA)**: The ADEA prohibits employment discrimination against individuals who are 40 years of age or older. This includes protection from age-based discrimination in hiring, firing, job assignments, promotions, compensation, and other terms and conditions of employment. Discriminatory actions based on age, like those George, Rose, and Anne faced, violate the ADEA.

- **Hostile Work Environment and Harassment**: Under the ADEA, harassment based on age, if severe enough to create a hostile or abusive work environment, is also prohibited. In Anne's case, Jake's repeated age-based comments might constitute age harassment, which the employer is obligated to address under the law.

- **Disparate Treatment**: When employees are treated differently because of their age, as George and Rose were in the context of career opportunities and promotions, it may constitute disparate treatment under the ADEA. This occurs when an employee is intentionally treated less favorably than others due to their age.

Summary:

In these cases, **George**, **Rose**, and **Anne** all experienced **age discrimination** or **age-related harassment**, which violates the **Age Discrimination in Employment Act (ADEA)**. In George's and Rose's cases, they were passed over for opportunities or excluded due to assumptions about their age, with younger employees being favored. Anne experienced harassment in the form of derogatory remarks about her age. In all cases, the employers' dismissive response to the employees' complaints and failure to take appropriate action exacerbated the discrimination, leaving the employees feeling unsupported and marginalized. These actions violate both the **ADEA** and the obligation of employers to provide a workplace free from age discrimination and harassment.

2.8 Religious Discrimination

Definition and Scope

- **Understanding Religious Discrimination**:
  - Religious discrimination occurs when individuals face unfair treatment based on their religious beliefs or practices. This can

impact various areas, including employment, education, and housing, leading to significant legal implications.

- **Legal Protections**:

  o The concept of religious freedom is enshrined in the First Amendment and further protected under laws like Title VII of the Civil Rights Act, which prohibits employment discrimination based on religion.

Accommodating Religious Practices

- **Religious Discrimination Overview:** Employees may face discrimination based on their religious beliefs or practices, which can manifest in negative stereotypes, harassment, or being denied opportunities due to their faith. This type of discrimination can lead to a toxic work environment and affect employee mental health.

- **Accommodating Religious Practices:** Employers are legally required to accommodate employees' religious practices unless doing so would impose an undue hardship on the business. Examples of reasonable accommodations can include flexible scheduling for religious observances, providing designated prayer spaces, or allowing for dress codes that respect religious attire. Failure to accommodate these needs can lead to discrimination claims and contribute to a non-inclusive work environment.

- **Building a Respectful Workplace:** Creating an environment that respects diverse religious beliefs not only helps in complying with legal obligations but also enhances workplace cohesion. Organizations can benefit from diversity training that promotes understanding and respect among employees of different faiths.

Key Legislation

- **Title VII of the Civil Rights Act:**

  o Title VII provides comprehensive protections against employment discrimination based on religion, ensuring that individuals can practice their faith without fear of retaliation or discrimination in the workplace.

- **First Amendment Rights**:

  - o The First Amendment includes both the Free Exercise Clause and the Establishment Clause, which protect individuals' rights to practice their religion and prevent the government from favoring one religion over another.

Key Case Studies

- **Employment Division v. Smith (1990)**:

  - o This case discussed the limits of religious practices in the workplace, highlighting the balance between individual rights and governmental interests in regulating employment.

- **Burwell v. Hobby Lobby Stores, Inc. (2014)**:

  - o This ruling affirmed the rights of closely held corporations to deny contraceptive coverage based on religious objections, raising questions about the intersection of corporate rights and religious freedom.

Current Issues

- **Discrimination Against Religious Minorities**:

  - o Religious minorities, including Muslims, Sikhs, and Jews, often face discrimination in various forms, including hate crimes and workplace bias. Addressing these challenges requires robust legal protections and community support.

- **Legislative Developments**:

  - o Ongoing legislative actions and court rulings continue to shape the landscape of religious discrimination, including discussions around accommodations in the workplace and public spaces.

Examples of Religious Discrimination

1. Scenario: Religious Discrimination and Harassment in the Workplace

The Incident:

Ahmed, a Muslim employee at a financial services firm, wears a hijab as part of his religious practice. During a team meeting, his colleague Sarah comments that Ahmed's attire is "not professional" and implies he isn't fit for client-facing roles because of it. Over the next few weeks, Sarah continues to make snide remarks about Ahmed's religious practices, including questioning his need for time off for religious holidays. Other team members notice but remain silent. Ahmed tries to address the issue directly with Sarah, asking her to stop, but she dismisses him and escalates her behavior by making more overtly derogatory remarks in front of others. Frustrated, Ahmed reports the harassment to HR, providing examples of Sarah's comments and explaining the hostile environment it creates. However, HR dismisses his concerns, suggesting that Sarah's comments are "friendly banter" and that Ahmed should not take them personally. HR fails to investigate or provide any support, leaving Ahmed feeling isolated and unsupported in the workplace.

Explanation:

Ahmed's experience may involve **religious discrimination** and **religious harassment**, both of which are prohibited under **Title VII of the Civil Rights Act of 1964**. Title VII protects employees from discrimination based on religion, including religious practices such as wearing religious attire (like the hijab) and requesting time off for religious holidays. Sarah's comments about Ahmed's attire being "unprofessional" and her questioning of his religious practices (e.g., time off for holidays) could constitute discriminatory remarks based on his religion. Additionally, Ahmed's efforts to address the issue directly with Sarah and HR's failure to intervene could be seen as a failure by the employer to provide a workplace free from religious harassment. HR's dismissive attitude towards his concerns further underscores the violation of his rights to work in a discrimination-free environment.

2. Scenario: Religious Discrimination in Time-Off Requests and Job Assignments

The Incident:

Maria, a Latina employee at a marketing agency, practices Christianity and regularly attends church on Sundays. She requests time off to celebrate Easter, but her manager, Tom, responds dismissively, stating, "We can't afford to have you out on such an important workday." Over the next few weeks, Maria notices that Tom assigns her less desirable tasks, implying that her commitment to the job is questionable because of her religious observances. During team meetings, Tom also makes sarcastic comments about "those who need to pray instead of working." Feeling marginalized, Maria documents the incidents and reports the discrimination to HR, providing specific examples of Tom's comments and how they negatively impact her work environment. However, HR brushes off her concerns, telling her that Tom is under pressure and that she should focus on her performance rather than his remarks. HR fails to investigate or address her complaints, leaving Maria feeling unsupported and demoralized in her role.

Explanation:

Maria's experience may involve **religious discrimination** under **Title VII of the Civil Rights Act of 1964**. Title VII prohibits discrimination based on religion, including aspects of religious observance such as taking time off for religious holidays like Easter. Tom's response to Maria's request for time off, as well as his assignment of less desirable tasks and sarcastic comments about her religious practices, may constitute discriminatory actions based on her religion. Employers are required to make reasonable accommodations for an employee's religious practices unless doing so would cause undue hardship to the business. In Maria's case, Tom's refusal to accommodate her religious observance (Easter) and the subsequent adverse treatment may be a violation of her rights under Title VII. Additionally, HR's failure to investigate her complaint or take corrective action reinforces the employer's disregard for Maria's protected rights under the law.

3. Scenario: Religious Harassment and Hostile Work Environment

The Incident:

Amina, a Muslim employee at a healthcare clinic, wears a hijab as part of her religious practice. Recently, her colleague Mark starts making uncomfortable jokes about her hijab during staff meetings, suggesting that she should "take it off to fit in" and questioning her choice to work there. Initially, Amina tries to ignore the comments, but they become more frequent. During a lunch break, Mark even implies that Amina should justify her attire to the rest of the team. Feeling targeted, Amina documents Mark's comments and reports them to HR, explaining how his behavior has made her feel unwelcome and uncomfortable. However, HR dismisses her complaint, stating that Mark is simply "trying to be funny" and that Amina should be more open to workplace humor. HR decides not to investigate further or provide any support, leaving Amina feeling isolated and disrespected in her workplace.

Explanation:

Amina's experience may involve **religious harassment** and a **hostile work environment** under **Title VII of the Civil Rights Act of 1964**. Harassment based on religion is prohibited when it creates a hostile work environment that interferes with an employee's ability to perform their job. In Amina's case, Mark's repeated comments about her hijab, including suggesting she take it off and questioning her choice to wear it, could be seen as religious harassment. These comments are not only discriminatory but could also make Amina feel unwelcome and unsafe in her workplace. Title VII requires that employers take action to prevent and address religious harassment. HR's failure to take Amina's complaint seriously or provide any form of investigation or support violates her right to a harassment-free workplace. By dismissing the complaint as "just humor," HR is failing to meet its legal obligations under Title VII to prevent religious harassment and ensure that employees are not subjected to discriminatory treatment based on their religion.

Key Legal Frameworks:

- **Title VII of the Civil Rights Act of 1964**: Title VII prohibits discrimination in the workplace on the basis of race, color, religion, sex, or national origin. This includes discrimination against employees for practicing their religion, including wearing religious attire (like a hijab) or requesting time off for religious holidays. Under Title VII, employees are also protected from harassment based on their religion, and employers are required to prevent or remedy any such harassment that creates a hostile or abusive work environment.

- **Religious Accommodation**: Title VII also requires employers to provide reasonable accommodations for an employee's religious practices unless doing so would impose an undue hardship on the employer. For example, employers must accommodate employees' requests for time off for religious observances unless it would significantly disrupt the workplace. The employer must also ensure that employees are not discriminated against or harassed for practicing their religion.

- **Religious Harassment**: Under Title VII, religious harassment occurs when an employee is subjected to unwelcome and offensive behavior because of their religion. If the harassment creates a hostile work environment or interferes with the employee's work performance, the employer is legally obligated to take corrective action.

Summary:

In these cases, **Ahmed**, **Maria**, and **Amina** all faced forms of **religious discrimination** or **religious harassment** under **Title VII of the Civil Rights Act of 1964**. Ahmed was subjected to discriminatory comments about his hijab, Maria was penalized for requesting time off for religious observances, and Amina faced harassment about her hijab and religious practices. In all cases, **HR's failure to investigate** or intervene in a timely and effective manner allowed these forms of discrimination and harassment to continue, further compounding the harm these employees experienced. These actions violate the **right to practice religion freely** in the workplace, and HR's dismissive responses failed to meet legal obligations to provide a discrimination-free work environment.

2.9 Genetic Information Discrimination

Definition and Scope

- **Overview of Genetic Discrimination:** Genetic information discrimination occurs when individuals face adverse treatment based on their genetic predispositions or hereditary characteristics. This can happen in various domains, including employment and health insurance. Genetic discrimination encompasses actions that unfairly disadvantage individuals due to their genetic traits or family history of certain medical conditions, rather than actual health status.

- **Legal Distinction:** It is important to differentiate between genetic predispositions—indications of potential health risks based on genetics—and actual medical conditions. Discrimination based on genetic predisposition can lead to negative consequences, such as being overlooked for job opportunities or denied insurance coverage. This legal distinction is critical as it highlights the preventative nature of discrimination based on future health risks rather than current health issues.

Historical Context

- **Evolution of Genetic Testing:** The journey of genetic testing began with the discovery of DNA's double helix structure in the 1950s. In the subsequent decades, advancements in biotechnology led to the development of genetic screening tools. By the 1990s, the Human Genome Project was initiated, aiming to map all human genes. This project not only enhanced our understanding of genetics but also raised ethical concerns about how genetic information could be used in society.

- **Early Instances of Discrimination:** Instances of genetic discrimination began surfacing as testing became more commonplace. For example, individuals with a family history of conditions like Huntington's disease or breast cancer often experienced job loss or denial of health insurance. Awareness of these cases prompted public advocacy for legislation that would protect individuals from such discrimination, laying the groundwork for future legal protections.

Protections Against Genetic Bias

- **Genetic Discrimination Overview:** Genetic discrimination occurs when an individual is treated unfairly because of information about their genetic predisposition to certain health conditions. This is prohibited under laws such as the Genetic Information Nondiscrimination Act (GINA), which protects individuals from discrimination in health insurance and employment.

- **Impact on Employment:** Employees may worry about disclosing genetic information for fear it could affect their job security or advancement opportunities. Employers must ensure that genetic information is kept confidential and that hiring and promotion decisions are based solely on relevant job qualifications, not genetic factors.

- **Raising Awareness:** Organizations should promote awareness of genetic discrimination and the protections in place to safeguard employees. Implementing training programs can help foster an understanding of the implications of genetic information and ensure compliance with applicable laws.

Legal Framework

- **Genetic Information Nondiscrimination Act (GINA):** Enacted in 2008, GINA was a significant step in protecting individuals from genetic discrimination. It consists of two primary titles:

  - **Employment Protections:** Title I prohibits employers from using genetic information in decisions regarding hiring, firing, or promotions. Employers cannot request, require, or purchase genetic information from employees or applicants, except under specific circumstances (e.g., family medical history as part of a wellness program).

  - **Health Insurance Coverage:** Title II prohibits health insurers from denying coverage or charging higher premiums based on genetic information. This ensures that individuals cannot be penalized for their genetic predispositions, which may be entirely outside their control.

- **Limitations of GINA:** Despite its strengths, GINA has limitations. It does not apply to life insurance, long-term care insurance, or disability insurance, leaving gaps in protection. Consequently, individuals may still face discrimination in these areas, where insurers can use genetic information to deny coverage or increase premiums.

Case Studies

- **Key Legal Cases:**

  - **Davis v. Fortis Benefits:** This case involved a woman whose employer denied her insurance coverage after she disclosed her family history of breast cancer. The court ruled that this constituted discrimination under GINA, emphasizing the law's importance in protecting individuals from such unfair treatment.

  - **Parker v. Columbia Pictures:** In this case, a job applicant was denied a position based on a genetic predisposition to a health condition. The court's decision reinforced the application of GINA in employment contexts and served as a critical precedent for future cases involving genetic discrimination.

- **Implications for Future Cases:** These cases highlight the necessity of legal protections and the importance of raising public awareness. They demonstrate how effective legal action can mitigate genetic discrimination and set a precedent for future litigation.

Contemporary Issues

- **Emerging Challenges:** Despite the protections established by GINA, challenges persist, including:

  - **Awareness and Enforcement:** Many individuals remain unaware of their rights under GINA, leading to underreporting of discrimination incidents. Greater efforts in education and outreach are essential to empower individuals to recognize and assert their rights.

  - **Technological Advancements:** Rapid advancements in genetic testing and data analytics raise ethical and legal concerns. For example, as more employers consider genetic testing as part of wellness programs, the potential for misuse of genetic information increases, creating new ethical dilemmas.

- **Privacy Concerns:** With the rise of direct-to-consumer genetic testing services, such as 23andMe and AncestryDNA, privacy concerns have intensified. Individuals must navigate the potential risks of sharing their genetic data, which may be used in ways they did not anticipate, including being sold to third parties or used for discriminatory practices.

Conclusion

- **Summary of Genetic Discrimination:** Genetic information discrimination presents complex challenges that threaten individuals' rights and healthcare access. While GINA provides crucial protections, gaps still exist, and public awareness remains low. Advocacy for stronger protections is needed to ensure that all individuals can safely access their genetic information without fear of discrimination.

- **Encouragement for Advocacy:** As technology evolves, it is imperative to advocate for continued legal protections and public education about genetic discrimination. By fostering a more informed and supportive environment, we can work towards preventing unfair treatment based on genetic information and promoting equitable access to healthcare and employment opportunities.

Examples of Genetic Information Discrimination

1. Scenario: Genetic Discrimination in Promotion Decisions

The Incident:

Eric, a 45-year-old IT specialist, has worked at a large software company for several years. After learning about a genetic predisposition to a hereditary health condition, he decides to keep this information private. During a health benefits meeting, HR emphasizes the importance of updating health information. Shortly after, Eric notices a shift in his supervisor Karen's behavior. She starts making comments about his "health risks" and suggests that he may not be suitable for high-stakes projects. When Eric applies for a promotion, he is informed that decision-makers have concerns about his "long-term viability" in the role. Despite his qualifications, Eric is passed over in favor of a younger colleague. Feeling discriminated against, Eric documents these interactions and approaches HR, expressing concerns about potential **genetic discrimination**. However, HR dismisses his claims, saying they do not see any evidence of wrongdoing and implying that the decisions were purely based on business needs. No action is taken to address Eric's concerns, leaving him feeling unsupported and marginalized.

Explanation:

Eric's situation may involve **genetic discrimination**, which is prohibited under the **Genetic Information Nondiscrimination Act of 2008 (GINA)**. GINA makes it illegal for employers to discriminate against employees or applicants based on their genetic information, including information about a family member's health history or an individual's own genetic testing results. In Eric's case, Karen's comments about his "health risks" and the subsequent concerns raised about his "long-term viability" due to his genetic predisposition may constitute discrimination based on genetic information. Despite his qualifications and experience, Eric was passed over for a promotion, which could be a direct result of his genetic information being used in decision-making. HR's failure to address these concerns and their dismissive response further suggests that they have not complied with GINA's protections. Employers are prohibited from using genetic information to make employment decisions, including decisions about promotions or suitability for high-stakes projects.

2. Scenario: Genetic Discrimination in Job Opportunities

The Incident:

Lauren, a 38-year-old laboratory technician at a pharmaceutical company, is well-respected for her contributions. After undergoing genetic testing as part of a health initiative, she discovers she has a genetic marker for a hereditary condition. Though she keeps this information private, she notices her supervisor Mark becoming more invasive, asking personal questions about her health and suggesting she might struggle with upcoming projects. When Lauren applies for a leadership role, she receives a rejection email citing a lack of "long-term reliability." Lauren later learns that Mark raised concerns about her ability to handle the role due to her genetic predisposition. Feeling unfairly treated, Lauren documents her experiences and approaches HR to discuss her concerns about potential genetic discrimination. However, HR brushes off her claims, stating that they cannot intervene in management decisions. They suggest that Lauren should work harder to demonstrate her reliability rather than focus on "personal matters," leaving her feeling undervalued and anxious about her future at the company.

Explanation:

Lauren's experience may involve **genetic discrimination** under **GINA**. As with Eric's case, Mark's concerns about Lauren's ability to handle the leadership role due to her genetic predisposition could constitute discrimination based on genetic information. GINA explicitly prohibits employers from using genetic information in employment decisions, including hiring, promotions, and job assignments. Mark's invasive questions about Lauren's health and his subsequent actions—raising concerns about her "long-term reliability" based on her genetic testing results—could be seen as discriminatory behavior. HR's dismissive response to Lauren's complaint and their suggestion that she "work harder" to prove her reliability, rather than addressing her concerns about genetic discrimination, is a violation of her rights under GINA. Employers must ensure that genetic information is not used to make decisions about promotions, job assignments, or any other employment-related matters. By failing to take action, HR is enabling an environment where genetic discrimination goes unchecked.

Key Legal Frameworks:

- **Genetic Information Nondiscrimination Act (GINA) of 2008**:

  GINA prohibits discrimination based on genetic information in both employment and health insurance. Under GINA, employers are prohibited from using genetic information (such as family health history or results from genetic tests) when making decisions about hiring, firing, promotions, job assignments, and compensation. The law also prohibits employers from requesting or requiring genetic testing from employees or applicants, and it restricts the disclosure of genetic information.

  - **Employment Protections under GINA**:

    Employers cannot make employment decisions based on an employee's genetic information, nor can they use genetic information to determine the employee's qualifications, long-term viability, or ability to perform certain job duties. This includes both genetic predispositions to health conditions and genetic testing results.

- **Discriminatory Actions Under GINA**:

  Discriminatory actions may include:

  - Making negative employment decisions (e.g., promotions, hiring, assignments) based on genetic predispositions or conditions.

  - Asking employees or job applicants invasive questions about their genetic makeup, family health history, or genetic testing.

  - Using genetic information in a way that directly impacts an employee's ability to work or their career trajectory.

Summary:

In both Eric and Lauren's cases, they faced **genetic discrimination** under **GINA**, which was not adequately addressed by their employer or HR. Eric was passed over for a promotion, with his supervisor expressing concerns about his "long-term viability" due to a genetic predisposition, and Lauren faced rejection for a leadership role due to concerns raised about her genetic health risks. Both employees were subjected to inappropriate questioning about their health and genetic makeup. In both cases, HR failed to intervene or take corrective action, leaving the employees unsupported in an environment that violated their rights under GINA. These actions could be seen as violations of **GINA's employment protections**, which prohibit genetic discrimination and ensure that employees' genetic information is not used against them in the workplace.

2.10 Intersectionality

Concept of Intersectionality

- **Definition**:
  - o Intersectionality refers to the interconnected nature of social categorizations such as race, gender, class, and others, creating overlapping systems of discrimination or disadvantage. Understanding intersectionality is essential for recognizing how different forms of discrimination can compound and affect individuals in unique ways.

Application in Discrimination Cases

- **Complex Experiences**:
  - o Individuals who belong to multiple marginalized groups often experience discrimination that cannot be understood by examining each identity in isolation. For example, a Black woman may face both racial and gender discrimination, necessitating an intersectional approach to her case.

- **Legal Implications**:
  - o Courts are increasingly recognizing the importance of intersectionality in discrimination cases, understanding that overlapping identities can create compounded barriers. This recognition can affect how cases are prosecuted and adjudicated.

Examples of Intersectional Discrimination

- **LGBTQ+ People of Color**:

    o LGBTQ+ individuals from racially marginalized backgrounds often face unique challenges, including discrimination based on both race and sexual orientation, which can limit access to resources and support.

- **Women with Disabilities**:

    o Women with disabilities may encounter discrimination that combines gender bias with ableism, leading to significant barriers in employment, healthcare, and social services.

Importance of Intersectionality in Advocacy

- **Inclusive Policies**:

    o Advocating for policies that consider intersectionality can lead to more effective solutions that address the needs of all individuals, particularly those facing multiple forms of discrimination.

- **Awareness and Education**:

    o Increasing awareness of intersectionality in advocacy efforts can promote understanding and empathy, fostering a more inclusive society that recognizes and values diversity.

Examples of Intersectional Discrimination

1. Scenario: Discrimination Based on Race and Sex in Promotion Decisions

The Incident:

Lucia, a Latina woman in her early thirties, works as a project manager at a tech company. Despite consistently receiving positive performance reviews and taking on additional responsibilities, she is passed over for a promotion in favor of several male colleagues with less experience. Lucia learns that the promotion will go to a white male colleague who has a history of undermining her contributions in meetings. When she approaches her supervisor, the supervisor mentions that while Lucia is a strong worker, she lacks the "leadership presence" the company is looking for. Lucia feels that her race and gender are contributing to this assessment, as her male counterparts, with similar or lesser qualifications, are not subject to the same scrutiny. Lucia overhears her supervisor saying they needed someone who would "fit in" with the predominantly male, white team, which further solidifies her belief that racial and gender biases are affecting her career advancement. Lucia files a formal complaint with HR, citing both race and sex discrimination.

Explanation:

Lucia's case may involve **intersectional discrimination**—discrimination based on both **race (Latina)** and **sex (female)**. Under **Title VII of the Civil Rights Act of 1964**, it is unlawful for employers to discriminate against employees based on sex, race, or ethnicity in hiring, firing, promotions, or other employment decisions. In this case:

- The **promotion denial** and the supervisor's comments about leadership presence could be masking discriminatory bias. The comment about needing someone to "fit in" with the team, which is predominantly male and white, suggests that Lucia's gender and ethnicity may have been factors in the decision, which violates Title VII.

- **Sex and racial discrimination** are prohibited under Title VII, and **intersectional discrimination** recognizes that the combination of multiple factors (e.g., being a Latina woman) can amplify the discrimination someone experiences.

By citing both race and sex discrimination, Lucia is legally protected from being denied advancement based on either factor, and her HR complaint could trigger an investigation into whether these biases have influenced her career progression.

2. Scenario: Discrimination Based on Disability and Race in Promotion Decisions

The Incident:

Terrance, a Black man in his late twenties with a visible mobility impairment, works as a software developer at a large tech firm. He is passed over for a promotion in favor of a less experienced colleague, and his supervisor expresses concerns about how his disability might affect team dynamics and customer interactions. When Terrance meets with HR, he learns the company has not made sufficient accommodations for him, such as accessible conference rooms and transportation options, leading to the perception that he cannot perform in a leadership role. HR comments that they need someone who can "represent the firm well," which Terrance interprets as discrimination against people with disabilities. Furthermore, a colleague makes derogatory comments about his wheelchair, implying that his disability makes him less suitable for leadership. Terrance files a formal complaint citing discrimination based on both **race and disability**.

Explanation:

Terrance's situation likely involves **discrimination based on race** and **disability**, both of which are prohibited under federal law:

- **Disability discrimination** is prohibited under the **Americans with Disabilities Act (ADA)**. Employers are required to provide reasonable accommodations to employees with disabilities, and they cannot make employment decisions based on an employee's disability unless it directly impacts their ability to perform the essential functions of the job. The fact that Terrance's employer did not provide adequate accommodations (e.g., accessible conference rooms) and used his disability as a factor in denying him a promotion may constitute a violation of the ADA.

- **Race discrimination** is also prohibited under **Title VII of the Civil Rights Act of 1964**, which protects employees from discrimination based on race in all aspects of employment, including promotions. The concern that Terrance would not "represent the firm well" due to his disability, along with the racial undertones of his exclusion from leadership opportunities, could be a form of **intersectional discrimination**.

- The **hostile work environment** created by his colleague's comments about his wheelchair further highlights a culture of discrimination that impacts both his race and disability status. Under the ADA and Title VII, employees are entitled to a workplace free from harassment based on disability and race.

Terrance's filing of a formal complaint is legally justified, as the company's actions could be seen as violating both the **ADA** and **Title VII** in failing to provide necessary accommodations and in using discriminatory factors to assess his suitability for a leadership role.

3. Scenario: Discrimination Based on Gender Identity and Sexual Orientation

The Incident:

Morgan, a transgender woman in her early thirties who identifies as bisexual, works as a marketing manager at a mid-sized advertising agency. She has been a strong advocate for LGBTQ+ inclusion and has launched several diversity initiatives at the company. When a senior management position becomes available, Morgan applies, confident in her qualifications. However, during the interview process, she perceives subtle signs of bias against her. She notices that her male counterparts receive enthusiastic support from the hiring panel, while she faces questions about her "fit" within the company's leadership culture, which she interprets as a reference to her gender identity and sexual orientation. After the interviews, Morgan learns the position is awarded to a less qualified male colleague. Feedback from HR indicates that while they acknowledge her contributions, they express concerns about her "fit" within the team, implying that her gender identity and sexual orientation were factors in their decision. Morgan files a formal complaint with HR, citing discrimination based on both **sex** (gender identity) and **sexual orientation**.

Explanation:

Morgan's case involves **discrimination based on sex (gender identity)** and **sexual orientation**, which are protected categories under federal law:

- **Gender identity discrimination** is prohibited under **Title VII of the Civil Rights Act** as interpreted by the **U.S. Supreme Court** in **Bostock v. Clayton County (2020)**, which ruled that discrimination based on gender identity is a form of sex discrimination. Morgan's gender identity as a transgender woman cannot be used as a basis for denying her career advancement, and her experiences during the interview process suggest she may have been discriminated against on these grounds.

- **Sexual orientation discrimination** is similarly prohibited under Title VII, as confirmed by the **Bostock ruling**, which clarified that discrimination based on sexual orientation also constitutes sex discrimination. In Morgan's case, her bisexuality should not have been a factor in the decision-making process regarding her promotion.

- The **"fit" comment** regarding Morgan's ability to integrate into the leadership team likely reflects a bias against her gender identity and sexual orientation. These factors cannot legally be used to exclude her from leadership roles or to undermine her qualifications.

Morgan is legally protected against both **gender identity** and **sexual orientation** discrimination under Title VII, and her formal complaint to HR is an appropriate step to address these concerns.

Key Legal Protections:

1. **Title VII of the Civil Rights Act of 1964**:

   o **Sex Discrimination**: Includes discrimination based on gender, gender identity, and sexual orientation. Under Title VII, it is illegal to discriminate against an employee based on their gender identity or sexual orientation.

   o **Race Discrimination**: Prohibits discrimination based on race, color, or national origin, which includes the intersectional experience of discrimination based on both race and sex.

   o **Hostile Work Environment**: Employees are protected from harassment and discriminatory behavior based on sex, race, and sexual orientation in the workplace.

2. **Americans with Disabilities Act (ADA)**:

   o Prohibits discrimination based on disability and requires employers to provide reasonable accommodations for employees with disabilities. This includes not making employment decisions based on an employee's disability unless it directly affects their job performance.

Conclusion:

In all three scenarios, employees faced discrimination based on their **intersectional identities** (e.g., race and gender, race and disability, gender identity and sexual orientation), which violates federal protections under **Title VII** and the **ADA**. These laws ensure that discrimination in employment—whether in promotions, hiring, or other employment decisions—based on race, sex, gender identity, sexual orientation, or disability is illegal. The failure of HR to properly address or investigate these claims exacerbates the discrimination and makes these employees more vulnerable to further unfair treatment. Filing formal complaints is a crucial legal step, and they should be thoroughly investigated under the protections provided by federal law.

Understanding intersectionality is crucial for addressing the complex nature of discrimination in contemporary society. By recognizing how various social categorizations—such as race, gender, and disability—interact, we can better grasp the unique challenges faced by individuals at these intersections. Cases like those of Sofia, Terrance, and Alex illustrate the compounded discrimination that arises from overlapping identities, emphasizing the need for an inclusive approach in legal and organizational practices.

As courts and advocacy groups increasingly acknowledge intersectionality, it becomes imperative to develop policies and frameworks that address the nuanced experiences of marginalized individuals. This commitment not only promotes equity but also fosters a more just society, where all individuals can thrive without the burden of intersecting biases. Ultimately, embracing intersectionality in advocacy and legal frameworks can lead to meaningful progress in combating discrimination and supporting the diverse tapestry of human experiences.

The next chapter will explore adverse actions in discrimination cases, examining what constitutes an adverse action and its significance in legal claims.

Chapter 3: Adverse Actions in Employment Discrimination

3.1 Definition of Adverse Action

Understanding Adverse Action:

An adverse action refers to any action taken by an employer or other entity that negatively affects an individual's employment or status. This can include actions such as termination, demotion, refusal to hire, failure to promote, or any other action that detrimentally impacts the individual's employment conditions.

Legal Significance:

In discrimination cases, the concept of adverse action is crucial for establishing whether discrimination has occurred. To prove discrimination, the individual must demonstrate that an adverse action was taken against them because of a protected characteristic, such as race, gender, age, or disability.

3.2 Examples of Adverse Actions

Termination:

Dismissal from employment is one of the most clear-cut examples of an adverse action. If an employee can show that their termination was based on discriminatory reasons, it strengthens their case significantly.

Suspension:

A suspension from work, especially if it is imposed more frequently or severely on certain individuals compared to others for similar infractions, can be an indication of discriminatory practices. If the reasons for the suspension are tied to an employee's protected characteristics, it may constitute an adverse action.

Demotion:

A demotion involves a reduction in rank or responsibilities, which can affect an employee's salary and career progression. If a demotion is linked to discriminatory practices, it constitutes an adverse action.

Refusal to Hire:

When a qualified candidate is not hired, particularly in favor of a less qualified candidate, it may be an indication of discriminatory practices. Documentation of qualifications and comparisons can help demonstrate discrimination in hiring.

Failure to Promote:

Denial of promotions, especially when a less qualified individual receives the position, can signal discrimination. A pattern of consistently overlooking certain groups for advancement opportunities is also a key indicator.

Denied Benefits:

When an employee is denied benefits that are available to others, such as health insurance, retirement benefits, or bonuses, it can indicate discriminatory practices. For instance, if a specific group is systematically excluded from receiving certain benefits, it may constitute an adverse action.

Denied Accommodations:

This includes the refusal to provide reasonable accommodations for individuals with disabilities or other specific needs. For example, if an employer fails to make necessary adjustments, such as flexible work hours or modified equipment, it can negatively impact the employee's ability to perform their job and constitutes discrimination.

Transfer:

An involuntary transfer to a less desirable position or location can signal discrimination, particularly if the transfer is based on an individual's protected characteristic rather than legitimate business reasons.

Lay off:

Layoffs that disproportionately affect certain groups, especially if they are based on discriminatory factors rather than performance or economic necessity, can constitute an adverse action.

Discipline:

Disciplinary actions taken against an employee for behavior that others engage in without consequence may indicate discrimination. For example, if only certain groups face harsh penalties for similar actions, it could point to biased treatment.

Denied Religious Accommodations:

Failure to provide reasonable accommodations for an employee's religious practices, such as flexible scheduling for prayer or dress code exceptions, can be a form of discrimination. This denial can adversely affect the employee's ability to observe their faith.

Unfavorable Work Conditions:

Changes in work conditions, such as increased scrutiny, reduced hours, or unfavorable assignments that are disproportionately applied to certain individuals can also be classified as adverse actions.

Harassment:

Any form of unwelcome conduct based on a protected characteristic that creates a hostile or intimidating work environment can be considered harassment. This includes verbal, physical, or visual conduct that is discriminatory in nature.

Retaliation:

Taking adverse action against an employee for reporting discrimination, participating in an investigation, or exercising their rights under employment law can constitute retaliation. This may include actions like demotion, termination, or harassment.

Hostile Work Environment:

Creating or maintaining a workplace that is hostile due to discriminatory remarks, actions, or policies can be considered an adverse action. This can affect an employee's ability to work effectively and may lead to resignation or other negative consequences.

Involuntary Change in Job Duties:

An unexpected and unfavorable change in job responsibilities, particularly if it is not in line with the employee's role and is based on discriminatory reasons, can signify adverse action.

Negative Performance Evaluations:

Providing unjustifiably negative performance reviews that disproportionately affect certain individuals may indicate bias. If these evaluations are not based on actual performance but rather on discriminatory factors, they can constitute an adverse action.

Reduced Hours or Pay:

Cutting an employee's hours or pay without a legitimate business reason, particularly if it targets a specific group, can be an indication of discrimination.

Isolation or Exclusion:

Deliberately isolating an employee from team activities, meetings, or decision-making processes can be a form of discrimination. This can create a sense of exclusion and negatively impact the individual's career growth.

Failure to Provide Training Opportunities:

Denying certain employees access to training, development programs, or professional growth opportunities based on discriminatory factors can hinder their career advancement.

Increased Scrutiny:

Subjecting certain employees to higher levels of oversight or criticism compared to their peers may indicate bias, particularly if this scrutiny is not based on performance-related issues.

Note on Adverse Actions

While the examples provided above highlight some common forms of adverse actions that can constitute discrimination, it is important to understand that this list is not exhaustive. Discrimination can manifest in various other ways, and adverse actions may differ depending on specific circumstances and contexts. Each case is unique, and adverse actions can encompass any behavior or practice that negatively impacts an individual's employment status or working conditions based on protected characteristics.

Additionally, new forms of discrimination may emerge as workplaces evolve and societal norms change. Therefore, it is crucial for individuals to remain vigilant and informed about their rights and to recognize that discrimination can take many forms, both overt and subtle. If you believe you have experienced an adverse action, it is advisable to consult with legal professionals or civil rights organizations to explore your options for addressing the situation.

3.3 The Role of Adverse Actions in Discrimination Claims

- **Establishing a Prima Facie Case:**

- Generally, to build a prima facie case for employment discrimination, a Complainant must show:

    1. They belong to a protected class.

    2. They were qualified for the employment.

    3. They experienced an adverse action.

    4. The adverse action was taken under circumstances that suggest discriminatory motives.

- If the employer then provides a rebuttal or legitimate business reason for the adverse action, then the Complainant must prove:

    5. There is evidence that the employer's stated reason for the action was a pretext for discrimination.

- It's important to note that the elements for a prima facie case may differ for a harassment claim, denied accommodations, and certain other claims, however this model is a common analysis used by the EEOC and other civil rights agencies for disparate treatment.

- **Connecting Adverse Actions to Discrimination**:

    - The Complainant must establish a causal link between the adverse action and the discriminatory motive. This often requires showing that similarly situated individuals outside the protected class were treated more favorably.

- **Burden of Proof**:

    - In discrimination cases, the burden of proof often shifts. Initially, the burden is on the Complainant to establish a prima facie case. Once established, the burden shifts to the employer to provide a legitimate, non-discriminatory reason for the adverse action.

3.4 Documentation of Adverse Actions

- **Importance of Evidence**:

- Documenting adverse actions is vital for substantiating claims. This includes gathering evidence such as performance reviews, email communications, witness statements, and any relevant policies or procedures that demonstrate a pattern of discrimination.

- **Types of Documentation**:

  - **Written Records**: Emails or memos that show discriminatory comments or actions can serve as crucial evidence.

  - **Performance Evaluations**: Reviews that indicate a pattern of bias, especially if they deviate from standard evaluations, can strengthen a claim.

  - **Comparative Evidence**: Records showing how similarly situated individuals outside of the protected class were treated can help establish discriminatory patterns.

3.5 Legal Remedies for Adverse Actions

- **Types of Legal Remedies Available**:

  - Individuals who successfully prove that an adverse action was taken against them due to discrimination may be entitled to various remedies, including:

    - **Reinstatement**: Returning the individual to their former position if they were wrongfully terminated or demoted.

    - **Back Pay**: Compensation for lost wages due to the discriminatory action.

    - **Compensatory Damages**: For emotional distress or other non-economic harms resulting from the adverse action.

    - **Punitive Damages**: In cases of particularly egregious conduct, punitive damages may be awarded to deter future violations.

3.6 Current Trends and Challenges

- **Changing Workplace Dynamics**:

- As workplaces evolve, so do the ways in which adverse actions manifest. Remote work, for example, has introduced new dynamics in how employees are managed and evaluated.

- **Emerging Issues**:

  - New forms of discrimination, such as those based on sexual orientation or gender identity, are increasingly coming to the forefront, leading to ongoing legal developments and challenges.

- **Awareness and Training**:

  - Employers are increasingly recognizing the importance of training on discrimination and adverse actions to prevent legal issues. Implementing comprehensive training programs can help mitigate the risk of discrimination claims.

In conclusion, adverse actions are pivotal in discrimination cases, as they serve as key indicators of unfair treatment based on protected characteristics. This chapter has outlined various forms of adverse actions, including termination, demotion, and denial of benefits, highlighting their legal significance in establishing claims of discrimination. Understanding these actions, along with the importance of thorough documentation and the evolving workplace dynamics, equips individuals with the knowledge needed to recognize and address discrimination effectively. By being informed about their rights and the potential remedies available, individuals can better advocate for themselves and contribute to a more equitable work environment.

This chapter has primarily addressed discrimination in the employment context. In the next chapter, we will shift our focus to discrimination in public accommodations, exploring the various ways individuals can face unfair treatment in these settings.

Chapter 4: Employer Legal Obligations in the Case of Workplace Discrimination

4.1 Legal Compliance and Best Practices

Employers have specific legal obligations to address discrimination in the workplace under federal, state, and local laws. These responsibilities are essential not only for legal compliance but also for fostering a fair and inclusive work environment. Below are the key responsibilities:

1. Develop and Enforce Anti-Discrimination Policies

Employers must establish clear, written anti-discrimination policies that prohibit discrimination and harassment based on protected characteristics, including but not limited to race, gender, age, disability, religion, sexual orientation, and national origin. These policies should outline what constitutes unacceptable behavior, the processes for reporting discrimination, and the consequences for violating these policies. It is crucial that these policies are communicated effectively to all employees, ensuring they understand their rights and the company's stance on discrimination.

2. Conduct Prompt Investigations

When an employee files a discrimination complaint, employers are legally required to conduct a prompt and thorough investigation. This involves gathering evidence, interviewing the Complainant, the accused, and any witnesses, and reviewing relevant documents or communications. The investigation should be impartial and objective, aiming to uncover the facts surrounding the complaint. Documentation of the entire investigative process, including interviews and findings, is essential to demonstrate compliance and due diligence.

3. Take Immediate Corrective Action

If the investigation reveals evidence of discrimination or harassment, employers must take appropriate corrective action. This could involve disciplinary measures against the offending party, which may range from reprimands to termination, depending on the severity of the behavior. Additionally, employers should consider implementing policy changes, providing additional training, or making adjustments to workplace practices to prevent future incidents. Ensuring that the affected employee feels supported is also a critical part of this process.

4. Provide a Safe Reporting Mechanism

Employers must establish a safe and confidential process for employees to report discrimination or harassment. This reporting mechanism should be easily accessible and clearly communicated to all employees. Importantly, employers must protect employees from retaliation for coming forward with complaints, as this is not only a legal requirement but also vital for encouraging a culture of openness and trust.

5. Offer Reasonable Accommodations

Under laws such as the Americans with Disabilities Act (ADA) and the Pregnancy Discrimination Act, employers are required to provide reasonable accommodations to employees with disabilities and those affected by pregnancy-related conditions, unless such accommodations would impose an undue hardship on the business. This may include modifications to work schedules, adjustments to job duties, or changes in the work environment to support the employee's needs.

6. Maintain Records

Employers should keep detailed records of all complaints, investigations, and actions taken in response to allegations of discrimination. This documentation is crucial for demonstrating compliance with legal obligations and can be invaluable in defending against any legal claims. Records should include the nature of the complaint, steps taken during the investigation, the findings, and any corrective actions implemented.

7. Train Employees

Employers are obligated to provide regular training for all employees, especially management, on discrimination laws, the company's policies, and how to recognize and prevent discrimination in the workplace. Training sessions should cover topics such as unconscious bias, respectful communication, and the importance of inclusivity. Ongoing education can help create a more informed workforce and reduce instances of discrimination.

By fulfilling these legal obligations, employers not only comply with the law but also contribute to a more respectful and inclusive workplace culture. This commitment to addressing discrimination can enhance employee morale, improve retention, and ultimately foster a more productive and innovative work environment.

4.2 Examples of an Employer Appropriately Addressing Discrimination

Example one

Background: Kim is a talented software developer at a tech company. She has been with the company for three years and consistently receives positive performance reviews. Recently, she announced her pregnancy to her manager, Tom. After her announcement, Kim begins to notice a shift in her treatment by Tom and some colleagues.

The Incident: In team meetings, Tom starts making comments suggesting that Kim might not be able to handle the demands of her role due to her pregnancy. He frequently implies that she should take a step back from high-profile projects to focus on her health. Other colleagues begin echoing these sentiments, and Kim feels increasingly sidelined. During a recent project review, Tom publicly questioned whether Kim would be able to meet deadlines, raising doubts about her commitment to the team.

Feeling uncomfortable and targeted, Kim documents her experiences and decides to approach HR to express her concerns about potential pregnancy discrimination.

HR Investigation:

1. **Initial Complaint:** Kim submits a formal complaint to HR, detailing the comments made by Tom and how they have impacted her work environment. She provides specific examples of his remarks and the changes in her project assignments.

2. **HR Response:** HR acknowledges receipt of the complaint and outlines the investigation process to Kim, ensuring her that the matter will be taken seriously and treated confidentially.

3. **Gathering Evidence:** HR conducts a thorough investigation, which includes:

   - **Interviews:** They interview Kim to gather more details about her experiences. HR also speaks with Tom, other team members, and any witnesses to understand the context and gather different perspectives.

   - **Reviewing Documentation:** HR reviews Kim's performance evaluations and any relevant emails or messages that could provide context to her claims.

4. **Finding Patterns:** During the investigation, HR uncovers a pattern of behavior where Tom's comments about Kim's pregnancy have influenced project assignments. Other employees confirm that they felt uncomfortable with Tom's remarks and noticed a change in Kim's role after her announcement.

5. **Conclusion:** Based on the findings, HR concludes that Tom's comments and actions constitute discrimination based on pregnancy, violating both company policy and the Pregnancy Discrimination Act.

Corrective Actions:

1. **Disciplinary Measures:** Tom receives a formal reprimand and is required to undergo training on pregnancy discrimination and workplace inclusivity.

2. **Policy Reinforcement:** The company revisits its anti-discrimination policies and provides a company-wide refresher training session on diversity, equity, and inclusion, emphasizing the importance of supporting pregnant employees.

3. **Support for Kim:** HR ensures that Kim is reinstated to her previous responsibilities with full support for any accommodations she may need during her pregnancy. They also provide her with a mentor to assist her with project management as she transitions back to her regular role.

4. **Ongoing Monitoring:** HR commits to monitoring the team dynamics to ensure that no further discrimination occurs, and that Kim feels supported in her work environment.

Outcome: Kim feels validated and supported by the company's response. The investigation not only addresses her immediate concerns but also fosters a more inclusive culture within the organization. The training sessions lead to a greater awareness among employees about the importance of diversity and the need to respect all employees, regardless of their personal circumstances.

This scenario illustrates a comprehensive and appropriate response to discrimination, highlighting the importance of timely action, thorough investigation, and effective communication in the workplace.

Example two

Background: Andre is a skilled data analyst at a financial firm, having worked there for four years with consistently high-performance reviews. Recently, he has noticed a change in his interactions with his manager, Lisa, and some colleagues following his promotion to a team lead role.

The Incident: After Andre's promotion, Lisa begins to make comments that undermine his authority, frequently questioning his decisions in front of the team. She suggests that Andre's leadership style may not resonate with clients, implying that he may lack the cultural understanding needed for the role. Other team members start echoing these sentiments, leading Andre to feel marginalized. During a meeting, Lisa publicly states that "not everyone can relate to our client base as effectively," suggesting that Andre's race might limit his effectiveness.

Feeling targeted and disheartened, Andre documents the incidents and approaches HR to report the potential racial discrimination he has experienced.

HR Investigation:

Initial Complaint: Andre files a formal complaint with HR, detailing the comments made by Lisa and how they have affected his work environment and professional reputation. He provides specific examples of her remarks and the changes in how his team members interact with him.

HR Response: HR acknowledges receipt of Andre's complaint and outlines the investigation process, assuring him that the matter will be handled confidentially and with the utmost seriousness.

Gathering Evidence: HR conducts a thorough investigation, which includes:

- **Interviews:** HR interviews Andre to gather more context about his experiences. They also speak with Lisa, team members, and other witnesses to obtain a range of perspectives.

- **Reviewing Documentation:** HR reviews Andre's performance evaluations and any relevant emails or meeting notes that might provide context to the situation.

- **Finding Patterns:** During the investigation, HR identifies a pattern of behavior in which Lisa's comments about Andre's leadership capabilities seem to correlate with his racial background. Other employees corroborate that they have felt uncomfortable with Lisa's remarks and have noticed a shift in Andre's role and treatment since his promotion.

Conclusion: Based on the investigation's findings, HR concludes that Lisa's comments and actions constitute racial discrimination, violating both company policy and the Civil Rights Act.

Corrective Actions:

- **Disciplinary Measures:** Lisa receives a formal reprimand and is required to undergo training on racial sensitivity and workplace inclusivity.

- **Policy Reinforcement:** The company revisits its anti-discrimination policies and organizes a company-wide training session focused on diversity, equity, and inclusion, stressing the importance of equitable treatment for all employees.

- **Support for Andre:** HR ensures that Andre is reinstated to his full responsibilities and provides him with additional resources, such as mentorship from a senior leader, to support his leadership development.

- **Ongoing Monitoring:** HR commits to monitoring team interactions to ensure that no further discrimination occurs, and that Andre feels supported in his role.

Outcome: Andre feels validated and supported by the company's response. The investigation effectively addresses his immediate concerns and promotes a more inclusive workplace culture. The training sessions increase awareness among employees about the significance of diversity and the necessity of respecting all colleagues, regardless of their background.

This scenario exemplifies a comprehensive and appropriate response to racial discrimination, underscoring the importance of timely action, thorough investigation, and effective communication in the workplace.

Example three

Background: Alicia is a dedicated marketing specialist at a large advertising agency. She has been with the company for over five years and is well regarded for her creativity and commitment. Recently, Alicia was diagnosed with a chronic health condition that requires her to manage her workload more carefully. She has communicated her need for flexible work arrangements to accommodate her treatment.

The Incident: After Alicia's diagnosis, her supervisor, Mike, begins to make comments that undermine her capabilities. In team meetings, he frequently suggests that Alicia may not be able to handle the pressures of upcoming projects due to her health condition. He implies that she should consider stepping back from high-profile campaigns, which leads to her feeling excluded and unsupported. During a project planning session, Mike publicly questions whether Alicia can meet the deadlines, raising concerns about her reliability.

Feeling marginalized and uncomfortable, Alicia documents these interactions and decides to approach HR to report her concerns regarding potential disability discrimination.

HR Investigation:

Initial Complaint: Alicia submits a formal complaint to HR, detailing Mike's comments and their impact on her work environment. She includes specific instances of his remarks and how her project responsibilities have changed since her diagnosis.

HR Response: HR acknowledges receipt of Alicia's complaint and explains the investigation process, assuring her that the matter will be taken seriously and treated confidentially.

Gathering Evidence: HR conducts a thorough investigation, which includes:

- **Interviews:** HR interviews Alicia to gain a deeper understanding of her experiences. They also speak with Mike, team members, and other relevant colleagues to gather different perspectives.

- **Reviewing Documentation:** HR examines Alicia's performance evaluations, any relevant emails, and meeting notes that may provide context to her claims.

- **Finding Patterns:** During the investigation, HR uncovers a pattern where Mike's comments about Alicia's health appear to influence her project assignments. Other employees confirm that they have felt uncomfortable with Mike's remarks and noticed a decrease in Alicia's involvement in key projects after her diagnosis.

Conclusion: Based on the findings, HR concludes that Mike's comments and actions constitute discrimination based on disability, violating both company policy and the Americans with Disabilities Act (ADA).

Corrective Actions:

- **Disciplinary Measures:** Mike receives a formal reprimand and is required to undergo training on disability awareness and inclusion in the workplace.

- **Policy Reinforcement:** The company reviews its anti-discrimination policies and conducts a company-wide training session on diversity, equity, and inclusion, emphasizing the importance of accommodating employees with disabilities.

- **Support for Alicia:** HR ensures that Alicia is reinstated to her original responsibilities with the necessary accommodations in place. They also connect her with resources such as an employee assistance program to support her health needs.

- **Ongoing Monitoring:** HR commits to monitoring team dynamics to ensure that no further discrimination occurs, and that Alicia feels supported in her work environment.

Outcome: Alicia feels validated and supported by the company's response. The investigation not only addresses her immediate concerns but also promotes a more inclusive culture within the organization. The training sessions lead to greater awareness among employees about the importance of supporting colleagues with disabilities and respecting their contributions.

This scenario illustrates a thorough and appropriate response to disability discrimination, highlighting the necessity of prompt action, comprehensive investigation, and effective communication in the workplace.

In conclusion, it is imperative for employers to take appropriate and immediate action when faced with discrimination in the workplace. Discrimination undermines not only the affected individuals but also the overall health of the organization. By conducting thorough investigations, implementing corrective measures, and fostering an inclusive culture, employers demonstrate their commitment to fairness, equality, and respect for all employees.

The next chapter will guide you through the essential steps of reporting discrimination, a crucial process in asserting your rights and seeking justice.

Chapter 5: Reporting Discrimination

When you encounter discrimination in the workplace, taking the right steps to report it is essential for both your well-being and the integrity of your work environment. This chapter offers a comprehensive guide on how to effectively report discrimination, focusing on initial responses, gathering necessary evidence, and navigating the reporting process.

5.1 Steps to Take When You Experience Discrimination

How to Approach the Situation Initially

1. **Stay Calm and Assess the Situation:**

   o It's natural to feel a rush of emotions after being the victim of discrimination, but try to take a moment to breathe deeply and collect your thoughts. Assessing the situation can help you determine the best course of action without reacting impulsively.

2. **Decide on Immediate Action:**

   o Depending on the severity of the incident, you may need to take immediate steps. If you feel threatened or unsafe, prioritize your safety and seek assistance from a trusted colleague, a supervisor, or even security personnel if necessary. In cases where you feel less threatened, you may choose to address the individual involved directly or report it to HR later.

3. **Document the Incident Promptly:**

   o As soon as you can, write down your account of what happened. Include the following details:

     - **Date and Time:** When the incident occurred.

     - **Location:** Where it took place.

     - **Individuals Involved:** Names of those directly involved, including any witnesses.

     - **Description of the Incident:** A clear, factual account of what was said or done, and any relevant context.

4. **Reach Out for Support:**

   o Talk to trusted colleagues or friends who can offer emotional support. Sharing your experience can help you feel less isolated and empower you to take action. Additionally, they may provide insight or advice based on their experiences, which can be valuable in determining your next steps.

Gathering Evidence and Documentation

1. **Collect Relevant Documentation:**

   o As you prepare to report the incident, gather all evidence related to the situation. This may include:

     - **Emails and Messages:** Any relevant correspondence that pertains to the incident, including emails, instant messages, or texts that demonstrate discriminatory behavior or comments.

     - **Reports or Memos:** Any internal documents that could help illustrate the context or the discriminatory practices.

     - **Witness Statements:** If colleagues witnessed the incident, ask if they would be willing to provide written accounts of what they saw or heard. These statements can significantly support your claims.

2. **Maintain a Detailed Incident Log:**

   o Continuously update your incident log with additional discriminatory actions or behaviors you experience. Keep track of:

     - **Recurring Incidents:** Note how often similar behaviors occur.

     - **Contextual Details:** Include information about what led up to the incident, as this can provide important context for your claims.

3. **Identify Witnesses:**

   o Make a list of individuals who witnessed the incident. Having witnesses can bolster your case significantly. Consider asking these individuals if they would be willing to support your account either informally or formally.

4. **Review Company Policies:**

   o Familiarize yourself with your company's policies on discrimination and harassment. Understanding your employer's procedures and protections can help you navigate the reporting process more effectively. Look for information on:

     - **Reporting Procedures:** How to file a complaint and to whom.

     - **Confidentiality Policies:** How your information will be handled during the investigation.

     - **Non-retaliation Policies:** Assurance that you won't face negative consequences for reporting discrimination.

5. **Prepare for Your Report:**

   o Before approaching HR or management, organize your documentation into a clear and concise format. Create a summary that highlights:

     - **What Happened:** A factual description of the discriminatory act.

     - **Impact on You:** How the incident affected your work, emotional well-being, or professional relationships.

     - **Steps Taken:** Any actions you have already taken, such as discussions with the individual involved or informal complaints made.

     - **Desired Outcomes:** Be clear about what you hope to achieve through your report (e.g., a formal investigation, changes in workplace policies, or a mediation process).

6. **Consider Legal Counsel:**

   o If you are uncertain about how to proceed or feel that your situation is particularly complex, consider consulting with a legal professional who specializes in employment law. An attorney can provide valuable insights tailored to your specific situation and help you understand your rights and options.

Reporting discrimination in the workplace is a crucial step not only for your own rights but also for fostering a healthier and more inclusive work environment. By approaching the situation thoughtfully and gathering comprehensive documentation, you empower yourself to advocate for your rights effectively. Remember that you are not alone; there are resources and support systems available to help you navigate these challenging situations. Taking action can lead to positive change, not just for yourself, but for your colleagues and the workplace as a whole. By standing up against discrimination, you contribute to a culture of accountability and respect that benefits everyone.

Once you've decided to report discrimination, it's crucial to know both the internal procedures your company has in place and the external options available to you. This chapter elaborates on those avenues, ensuring you're equipped to take informed action.

5.2 Internal Reporting Procedures

Understanding Your Company's Grievance Process

1. **Familiarize Yourself with Company Policies:**

   o Your employee handbook is a valuable resource. It often contains:

      - **Grievance procedures:** Detailed steps for filing complaints.

      - **Definitions of discrimination:** Specific examples tailored to your workplace.

      - **Reporting channels:** Information on whom to contact, including HR, supervisors, or designated complaint officers.

      - **Confidentiality assurances:** An outline of how your information will be protected during the investigation process.

2. **Know Your Rights:**

   o It's essential to understand your legal protections within the grievance process. Familiarize yourself with:

      - **Non-retaliation policies:** Protections against any adverse actions taken against you for reporting discrimination.

      - **Right to a fair investigation:** Assurance that your complaint will be taken seriously and investigated thoroughly.

3. **Identify Key Contacts:**

   o Before reporting, know who you should approach:

- **Human Resources (HR):** Typically the primary contact for reporting discrimination.

- **Direct Supervisors:** In some cases, reporting directly to your supervisor may be appropriate.

- **Diversity Officers or Compliance Officers:** These individuals may have specialized training in handling discrimination claims.

4. **Review Procedures:**

   o Make sure you understand the steps involved in the grievance process. This may include:

     - **Submitting a formal complaint:** Know if this requires a specific format or form.

     - **Initiating meetings:** Some companies may require an initial discussion before filing a formal complaint.

     - **Follow-up procedures:** Understand what to expect after your report is submitted, including timelines for investigations.

5.3 How to Prepare for Meetings with HR or Management

1. **Gather Your Documentation:**

   o Prepare to present evidence that supports your claims:

     - **Incident logs:** Detailed accounts of discriminatory actions.

     - **Supporting documents:** Emails, memos, or other records that corroborate your experience.

     - **Witness statements:** Accounts from colleagues who may have observed the discriminatory behavior.

2. **Create a Summary Statement:**

   o Develop a concise summary of your experiences:

     - **Overview of incidents:** Highlight key events that illustrate the discrimination.

- **Impact on you:** Explain how the incidents have affected your work and well-being.
- **Desired outcomes:** Be clear about what you hope to achieve from your report (e.g., a resolution, policy change, or disciplinary action).

3. **Practice Your Presentation:**

   o Rehearse what you plan to say in your meeting:

   - **Clarity and composure:** Focus on being clear and calm when discussing your experiences.
   - **Role-playing:** Consider practicing with a trusted colleague to refine your presentation.

4. **Plan for Questions:**

   o Anticipate questions that HR may have:

   - **Clarifications on incidents:** Be prepared to provide additional context or details.
   - **Previous actions taken:** Explain any informal steps you may have attempted prior to the formal report.

5. **Follow Up in Writing:**

   o After your meeting, send a summary email:

   - **Recap of the discussion:** Document what was discussed, agreements made, and any next steps outlined.
   - **Confirmation of understanding:** Reinforce your commitment to the process and any expectations set during the meeting.

5.4 External Reporting

How to File a Complaint with the EEOC or Local Agencies

1. **Understanding Your Options:**

   o If internal channels do not resolve your concerns, you can file a complaint with the EEOC or local agencies:

- **EEOC (Equal Employment Opportunity Commission):** Handles complaints about workplace discrimination at the federal level.

- **State and Local Agencies:** Many states have their own agencies that enforce anti-discrimination laws, often with additional protections.

2. **Filing a Charge with the EEOC:**

   o To initiate a complaint with the EEOC, follow these steps:

   - **Contact the EEOC:** You can file a charge online, by phone, or in person at a local EEOC office.

   - **Complete Required Forms:** Provide detailed information about the discrimination experienced, including:

     - The nature of the discriminatory act.

     - The dates and times of incidents.

     - Names of individuals involved.

     - Any witnesses present.

   - **Submit Supporting Documentation (Optional):** Include relevant evidence that supports your case.

3. **State and Local Agencies:**

   o In addition to the EEOC, research state and city agencies:

   - **State Laws:** Each state has different laws and protections. Research your local laws to ensure you understand the options available to you.

   - **Filing Procedures:** These may differ from federal procedures; familiarize yourself with what is required at the state level.

5.5 Time Limits for Filing Complaints

1. **Know the Deadlines:**

   o Time limits for filing complaints vary significantly:

- **EEOC Complaints:** Generally, you must file a charge within 180 days of the alleged discriminatory act. This period may extend to 300 days if a state or local anti-discrimination law is involved.
- **State Agencies:** Local timelines may differ, so check specific requirements for your state.

2. **Importance of Timely Reporting:**
   - Understanding and adhering to these deadlines is critical:
     - **Loss of Rights:** Missing these deadlines can result in the loss of your right to pursue legal action. Make it a priority to file as soon as possible.

3. **Consider Seeking Legal Advice:**
   - If you have questions about the filing process or the specifics of your situation, consider consulting with an employment law attorney:
     - **Guidance on Rights:** They can provide clarity on your rights and help you navigate the complaint process effectively.
     - **Assistance with Documentation:** Legal counsel can also help you gather and organize your documentation for a stronger case.

Reporting discrimination, whether internally or externally, is a crucial step in advocating for your rights and fostering a healthier workplace environment. By understanding internal procedures and knowing how to navigate external agencies, you empower yourself to take effective action. Remember, you have the right to a workplace free from discrimination, and there are resources available to support you in your pursuit of justice. Taking these steps not only helps you but also contributes to creating a fair and equitable work environment for all employees. By standing up against discrimination, you can initiate positive change and set a precedent for accountability and respect within your organization.

Once you have filed a complaint—whether internally with your organization or externally with the EEOC or local agencies—it's essential to understand what to expect during the investigation process. The next section provides an overview of the steps involved in an investigation and the potential outcomes you might encounter.

5.6 What to Expect During the Investigation Process

Overview of the Investigative Steps

1. **Initial Review of the Complaint:**

   - **Assessment:** Upon receiving your complaint, the HR department or external agency will conduct an initial review to determine if the complaint falls within their jurisdiction and if there is enough information to proceed.

   - **Acknowledgment:** You should receive a confirmation that your complaint has been received and is being reviewed.

2. **Investigation Planning:**

   - **Assigning an Investigator:** A designated investigator will be assigned to your case, often someone trained in handling discrimination claims.

   - **Developing an Investigation Plan:** The investigator will outline the steps needed to gather evidence, which may include interviewing relevant parties and reviewing documentation.

3. **Collecting Evidence:**

   - **Interviews:** The investigator will conduct interviews with you, the accused, and any witnesses you may have identified. Be prepared to:

     - **Explain your perspective:** Clearly articulate the events and context of the discrimination you experienced.

     - **Provide additional documentation:** Share any further evidence that supports your claims.

4. **Document Review:**

   - **Examining Company Records:** The investigator may review company policies, emails, performance evaluations, and other relevant documents to understand the context and assess the validity of the complaint.

- o **Analyzing Previous Complaints:** In some cases, the investigator might look into any prior complaints against the accused or related patterns of behavior within the organization.

5. **Conclusion of the Investigation:**

   - o **Final Report:** After collecting all evidence, the investigator will compile a report summarizing findings, which will typically include:

     - **Findings of fact:** A detailed account of the evidence gathered.

     - **Determination:** An assessment of whether discrimination occurred based on the evidence.

6. **Review and Recommendation:**

   - o **Internal Review:** The report may be submitted to HR or upper management for further review. They will determine any necessary actions based on the findings.

   - o **Recommendations:** The investigator may suggest remedial actions, policy changes, or disciplinary measures, depending on the severity of the findings.

5.7 Potential Outcomes of the Investigation

1. **No Violation Found:**

   - o If the investigation concludes that there was no evidence of discrimination, you will be informed of the findings. This outcome may include:

     - **Explanation of Findings:** The investigator will typically provide a rationale for their decision.

     - **No Further Action:** The organization may choose not to take any further action regarding the complaint.

2. **Violation Found:**

   - o If discrimination is substantiated, the organization may take various actions, including:

     - **Corrective Action:** This could involve retraining, implementing new policies, or changing work assignments.

- **Disciplinary Measures:** The accused may face disciplinary actions, which could range from a warning to termination, depending on the severity of the offense.

3. **Mediation or Settlement:**

   o In some cases, parties may be encouraged to engage in mediation to resolve the issue amicably. This process may include:

     - **Facilitated Discussions:** A neutral third party will assist both parties in reaching a mutually agreeable resolution.

     - **Compensation or Remedial Actions:** Solutions may involve compensation, changes in workplace conditions, or other agreements beneficial to the complainant.

4. **Right to Appeal:**

   o If you are dissatisfied with the outcome, many organizations have an appeal process in place:

     - **Filing an Appeal:** You can request a review of the findings, typically through a formal process outlined in your company's policies.

     - **Grounds for Appeal:** Clearly outline your reasons for appealing, such as new evidence or perceived bias in the investigation.

5. **Follow-Up:**

   o Regardless of the outcome, a follow-up meeting may be scheduled to discuss:

     - **Next Steps:** Clarifying any actions that will be taken moving forward.

     - **Support Resources:** Information on additional resources available to you, such as counseling or employee assistance programs.

Conclusion

Understanding the investigation process is crucial for navigating your complaint effectively. Being aware of the steps involved and the potential outcomes can help set realistic expectations and prepare you for any responses from your organization or external agencies. By remaining engaged and informed throughout the investigation, you can advocate for your rights and contribute to a culture of accountability within your workplace. Remember, reporting discrimination is a courageous step toward creating a fair and equitable work environment for yourself and others.

The next chapter will explain your rights during the investigation process after reporting workplace discrimination. You'll learn what to expect, how to protect yourself from retaliation, and how to engage with investigators effectively. This chapter will also cover potential outcomes and remedies, empowering you to navigate the process with confidence and ensure your rights are upheld.

Chapter 6: Your Rights During the Investigation

When you report discrimination in the workplace, it's essential to be aware of your rights during the subsequent investigation. This chapter provides an in-depth exploration of the fundamental rights you hold as an employee, ensuring you are well-informed and empowered to navigate the investigation process effectively.

6.1 Your Rights During the Investigation

Employee Rights During an Investigation

The Right to Confidentiality

1. **Understanding Confidentiality:**

   o Employees have a right to expect that their complaints will be handled confidentially to the maximum extent possible. This includes:

      - **Protection of Identity:** Your name and any identifying details should be kept private from other employees, especially the accused, unless disclosure is necessary for the investigation.

      - **Sensitive Information:** Any specific details about your complaint, including dates, incidents, and individuals involved, should also be protected from unauthorized disclosure.

2. **Importance of Confidentiality:**

   o Confidentiality is crucial for several reasons:

      - **Encouragement to Report:** When employees believe their complaints will remain confidential, they are more likely to report discrimination without fear of retribution or stigma.

      - **Maintaining Workplace Harmony:** Protecting the identity of complainants helps to prevent a hostile work environment and promotes trust among colleagues.

3. **Understanding Limitations:**

- While confidentiality is a right, there are certain limitations:
  - **Legal Obligations:** Employers may be required to disclose certain information to comply with laws or regulatory obligations, such as reporting patterns of discrimination to governmental agencies.
  - **Necessary Disclosure for Investigation:** To investigate thoroughly, some information may need to be shared with individuals who are directly involved in resolving the complaint.

4. **Discussing Concerns:**
   - If you have concerns about confidentiality, it's important to discuss them with HR or the investigator:
     - **Clarify Procedures:** Ask how your information will be safeguarded throughout the investigation and who will have access to it.
     - **Request Options:** Inquire about the possibility of anonymous reporting or measures that can be taken to protect your identity further.

The Right to Representation

1. **Understanding Your Right to Representation:**
   - You have the right to have a representative present during any part of the investigation process, which can include:
     - **Union Representation:** If you are a union member, you can bring a union representative to any meetings or interviews related to the investigation.
     - **Legal Counsel:** You may also choose to consult with or have an attorney accompany you, particularly if you anticipate potential legal implications.

2. **Role of Representation:**
   - Having representation can provide several advantages:

- **Guidance on Your Rights:** A representative can help ensure you understand your rights and the procedures involved in the investigation.

- **Assistance with Communication:** They can help articulate your concerns more effectively and ensure that your perspective is adequately represented.

- **Emotional Support:** Navigating the investigation can be stressful, and having someone you trust present can alleviate some anxiety.

3. **Notification of Representation:**

   o It's advisable to inform the investigator or HR in advance if you intend to bring a representative:

   - **Advance Notice:** Let them know your choice of representative before meetings to facilitate the process.

   - **Clarifying Participation:** Be clear about what role your representative will play during meetings—whether they will simply support you or actively participate in discussions.

4. **Limits on Representation:**

   o While you have the right to representation, there may be some limitations regarding their involvement:

   - **Scope of Participation:** Investigators may specify whether your representative can ask questions, speak on your behalf, or only provide silent support.

   - **Confidentiality Agreements:** Your representative may need to sign a confidentiality agreement to protect the integrity of the investigation and ensure that sensitive information is not disclosed outside of the process.

Additional Rights During the Investigation

1. **The Right to a Fair Investigation:**

   o You are entitled to a thorough and impartial investigation:

- **Impartiality:** The investigator must remain neutral, objectively examining all evidence without bias toward either party.
- **Thorough Evidence Collection:** The investigation should encompass gathering all relevant evidence, including documents, communications, and witness statements.

2. **The Right to Be Informed:**

   o You have the right to be kept informed about the investigation's progress:

   - **Regular Updates:** The investigator or HR should communicate with you regarding the status of your complaint, including any significant developments.
   - **Timeline Awareness:** You should be informed of an estimated timeline for the investigation, helping you understand when you can expect updates.

3. **Protection Against Retaliation:**

   o It is your right to be protected from retaliation for filing a complaint or participating in an investigation:

   - **Legal Protections:** Federal and state laws protect employees from any adverse actions taken as a result of their complaints, including demotion, termination, or harassment.
   - **Reporting Retaliation:** If you experience retaliation, document these incidents and report them immediately to HR or the appropriate authority, such as the agency you filed a complaint with, as retaliation can lead to further legal consequences for the employer.

4. **The Right to a Safe Environment:**

   o Employees have the right to feel safe and secure in the workplace:

   - **Support During the Process:** Employers should ensure that you are not subjected to a hostile work environment during the investigation.
   - **Adjustments If Necessary:** If you feel unsafe, you can request adjustments to your work situation, such as a temporary

transfer or change in reporting lines, until the investigation concludes.

5. **The Right to Seek Legal Counsel:**

   o You have the right to seek advice from a lawyer regarding your situation:

     ▪ **Understanding Legal Rights:** Consulting with legal counsel can provide clarity on your rights, the potential outcomes of your complaint, and the implications of the investigation.

     ▪ **Preparation for Possible Outcomes:** A lawyer can help you prepare for any potential legal proceedings that may arise from your complaint.

Being aware of your rights during an investigation is crucial for effectively navigating the process and ensuring that your voice is heard. By understanding your rights to confidentiality, representation, and protection against retaliation, you can advocate for yourself confidently. Remember that the investigation is designed to promote fairness and accountability in the workplace, and knowing your rights will empower you to seek justice while fostering a healthier work environment for all employees. Your courage in standing up against discrimination is a vital step towards creating an equitable workplace.

6.2 Understanding Confidentiality and Retaliation Protections

When you take the important step of reporting discrimination in the workplace, understanding your rights regarding confidentiality and retaliation protections is crucial. This section will provide a comprehensive overview to ensure you are fully informed as you navigate this process.

Understanding Confidentiality

1. **Legal Definition of Confidentiality:**

   o Confidentiality in the workplace refers to the ethical and legal obligation of employers to protect the privacy of employees who report discrimination or harassment. Key elements include:

     ▪ **Protected Information:** Any details relating to your identity as a complainant, the nature of your complaint, and any statements made during the investigation should be safeguarded.

- **Controlled Access:** Information should only be disclosed on a need-to-know basis, limited to individuals directly involved in the investigation or resolution process.

2. **Importance of Confidentiality:**
   - The maintenance of confidentiality serves multiple vital purposes:
     - **Encouraging Reporting:** When employees know that their complaints will be treated confidentially, they are more likely to report incidents of discrimination without fear of personal or professional repercussions.
     - **Trust in the System:** Confidentiality fosters a sense of trust between employees and management, creating a safer environment for open dialogue about workplace issues.

3. **Limitations on Confidentiality:**
   - While confidentiality is critical, it is essential to understand its limitations:
     - **Investigative Requirements:** In some cases, the nature of an investigation may require sharing certain details with other employees, including the accused, though this should be handled delicately and with prior notice where possible.
     - **Legal Obligations:** Employers may be compelled to disclose certain information for legal compliance, such as reporting to regulatory agencies or during legal proceedings.

4. **Addressing Confidentiality Concerns:**
   - If you have specific concerns about how your information will be handled, consider the following steps:
     - **Open Dialogue with HR:** Before filing a complaint, discuss your concerns about confidentiality with your HR representative. Ask about the protocols in place to protect your information.
     - **Request Written Policies:** Ask for documentation outlining the company's confidentiality policies regarding investigations. Knowing what the organization commits to can give you peace of mind.

- **Establish Expectations:** Communicate your expectations for confidentiality clearly when you file your complaint, reinforcing the importance of protecting your identity throughout the process.

Retaliation Protections

1. **Legal Protections Against Retaliation:**
   - Both federal and state laws offer strong protections against retaliation for employees who report discrimination:
     - **Title VII of the Civil Rights Act:** This landmark legislation prohibits employers from retaliating against employees for asserting their rights under anti-discrimination laws.
     - **Other Federal Laws:** The Americans with Disabilities Act (ADA), Age Discrimination in Employment Act (ADEA), and the Equal Pay Act also provide specific protections against retaliation related to their respective areas of focus.
     - **State-Level Protections:** Many states have enacted laws that offer even broader protections against retaliation, which may cover additional forms of discrimination or extend to employees in certain protected classes.

2. **What Constitutes Retaliation?**
   - Retaliation can manifest in various forms, and understanding these can help you recognize if you're facing unfair treatment:
     - **Adverse Employment Actions:** This can include demotions, dismissals, changes in work assignments, or reductions in pay that occur as a direct response to your reporting.
     - **Hostile Work Environment:** Even if formal employment actions are not taken, retaliation can include ongoing harassment, bullying, or ostracization by colleagues or supervisors as a form of punishment for speaking out.
     - **Denial of Benefits:** Retaliation may also involve denying promotions, raises, or access to training opportunities that are available to other employees.

3. **Reporting Retaliation Incidents:**

   o If you believe you are experiencing retaliation after reporting discrimination, take the following steps:

      - **Document Everything:** Keep detailed records of any incidents of retaliation, including:

         - **Dates and Times:** Note when each incident occurred.

         - **Descriptions of Events:** Write a clear account of what happened, who was involved, and any witnesses present.

         - **Communications:** Save any emails, messages, or written communications related to the retaliation.

      - **Internal Reporting:** Approach your HR department or a trusted supervisor to report the retaliatory behavior:

         - **Present Your Evidence:** Share the documentation you've gathered, outlining your concerns and the timeline of events clearly.

         - **Request an Investigation:** Ask HR to investigate the retaliatory actions and address your concerns promptly.

      - **External Reporting to Regulatory Agencies:** If internal resolution efforts do not yield results:

         - **File a Complaint with the EEOC:** You can file a charge with the Equal Employment Opportunity Commission (EEOC) or a state agency responsible for enforcing employment laws. Be mindful of time limits for filing these complaints, which typically range from 180 to 300 days from the date of the retaliatory act.

4. **The Role of Legal Counsel:**

   o Seeking legal counsel can be invaluable in the event of retaliation:

      - **Consultation for Clarity:** An attorney specializing in employment law can help you understand your rights, evaluate your case, and outline potential next steps.

- **Legal Representation:** If necessary, a lawyer can represent you in dealings with your employer or in any legal proceedings that may arise, providing you with expert guidance throughout the process.

5. **Creating a Safe Work Environment:**

   o It's essential for employers to foster a workplace culture that prioritizes confidentiality and protects against retaliation:

      - **Training and Education:** Organizations should implement regular training for employees and management on discrimination, harassment, and retaliation to promote awareness and compliance with legal standards.

      - **Clear Reporting Channels:** Establish and communicate clear protocols for reporting discrimination and retaliation, ensuring employees know how to safely voice their concerns.

      - **Support Systems:** Employers should offer resources such as counseling services or hotlines to assist employees facing discrimination or retaliation, demonstrating a commitment to a safe and supportive work environment.

Understanding your rights to confidentiality and protection against retaliation is crucial as you navigate the process of reporting workplace discrimination. By being informed about these rights, you can advocate for yourself effectively and ensure that your concerns are addressed appropriately. Remember, standing up for your rights not only benefits you but also contributes to a healthier, more equitable workplace for all employees. If you encounter issues with confidentiality or retaliation, don't hesitate to seek support from trusted colleagues, HR, or legal professionals to protect your interests and well-being. Your courage in addressing discrimination is vital to fostering a culture of respect and fairness in the workplace.

6.3 Outcomes of Investigations

Understanding the potential outcomes of an investigation into workplace discrimination is crucial for employees who have reported such incidents. This section will explore the different resolutions that may arise from the investigation process, as well as the options available if you find the outcome unsatisfactory.

Possible Resolutions

1. **Settlement Agreements:**

   o **Nature of Settlements:**

      - Settlement agreements often represent a compromise between the employee and employer. These agreements can involve:

         - **Financial Compensation:** The employer may agree to provide monetary compensation for damages or losses incurred due to discrimination, which could cover lost wages, emotional distress, and related expenses.

         - **Policy Changes:** Your settlement terms may include commitments to change discriminatory practices or implement new policies designed to prevent future incidents, ensuring a safer workplace for all employees.

         - **Non-Disclosure Agreements:** Often, settlements will require confidentiality regarding the terms, preventing the employee from discussing the details publicly. This protects the company's reputation while ensuring the employee receives the necessary compensation or resolution.

2. **Policy Changes:**

   o **Impact of Policy Changes:**

      - One of the most impactful outcomes of an investigation can be the implementation of new policies or the revision of existing ones. This may involve:

         - **Enhanced Training Programs:** Employers may establish or strengthen training programs focused on diversity, inclusion, and preventing discrimination. Such programs should educate employees about recognizing discriminatory behavior and foster a culture of respect.

         - **Clearer Reporting Procedures:** Organizations might revise their grievance procedures to make it easier for employees to report issues safely and confidentially.

This can include the establishment of anonymous reporting channels or dedicated hotlines.

- **Stricter Enforcement of Anti-Discrimination Policies:** Changes may also include more rigorous enforcement of existing anti-discrimination policies, with established consequences for violations. Employers should communicate these policies effectively to all staff members.

3. **Disciplinary Actions:**

   o **Nature of Disciplinary Actions:**

   - If the investigation substantiates the complaint, disciplinary actions may be taken against those found responsible for discriminatory behavior. These actions can range from:

     - **Warnings or Reprimands:** Minor violations may result in verbal or written warnings, outlining the nature of the violation and potential consequences for future incidents.

     - **Suspension:** More serious offenses might lead to temporary suspension from work, allowing the employer to assess the situation without the offending employee's presence.

     - **Termination:** In cases of severe or repeated violations, the employer may choose to terminate the employment of the offending party, thereby sending a clear message that discrimination will not be tolerated.

4. **Training and Education Initiatives:**

   o **Focus on Education:**

   - As a direct outcome of the investigation, employers may initiate training programs aimed at educating employees about discrimination, harassment, and inclusivity. This could involve:

     - **Workshops and Seminars:** Regular training sessions to reinforce company values, educate employees on their rights, and promote a respectful workplace. These sessions can include role-playing scenarios to help employees identify and respond to discriminatory behavior.

- **Resource Materials:** Distribution of handbooks or materials that outline employee rights and the importance of a discrimination-free environment, ensuring that all employees have access to critical information.

5. **Formal Communication:**

   o **Communication of Findings:**

      - After concluding the investigation, employers may provide formal communication detailing the findings and the actions taken. This can include:

         - **Summary Reports:** A written summary outlining the investigation process, findings, and any actions taken. This transparency helps build trust in the process.

         - **Follow-Up Meetings:** Opportunities for employees to discuss the outcome and any further concerns with HR or management, ensuring that employees feel heard and valued.

6.4 Next Steps if Unsatisfied with the Outcome

If you are not satisfied with the outcome of the investigation, it is essential to know the options available to you:

1. **Requesting a Review:**

   o **Formal Review Process:**

      - You may have the right to request a review of the investigation's findings or the resolution. Steps to consider include:

         - **Submitting a Formal Request:** Contact HR or the designated individual handling your complaint to formally request a review or appeal of the findings.

Ensure that your request is documented in writing to maintain a record.

- **Providing Additional Evidence:** If new information or evidence has come to light since the investigation concluded, present this information to support your request, which could influence the outcome of the review.

2. **Pursuing Internal Grievance Procedures:**

   o **Escalating Complaints:**

   - Many organizations have internal processes for escalating complaints. This might involve:

     - **Filing an Appeal:** Follow your company's established procedures for appealing the investigation outcome. Be clear about why you believe the initial decision was incorrect or insufficient.

     - **Escalating to Higher Management:** If HR's response is unsatisfactory, consider escalating the issue to higher-level management or executives within the organization. Prepare a concise summary of your concerns and previous communications for clarity.

3. **Contacting Regulatory Agencies:**

   o **Filing External Complaints:**

   - If internal options do not lead to a satisfactory resolution, you may file a complaint with external regulatory bodies, such as:

     - **Equal Employment Opportunity Commission (EEOC):** You can file a charge with the EEOC if you believe your discrimination complaint was not adequately addressed. Be mindful of the time limits for filing these complaints, which typically range from 180 to 300 days from the date of the discriminatory act.

     - **State Labor Departments:** Many states have agencies that handle discrimination complaints, which may provide additional avenues for recourse. Research the specific laws and processes applicable in your state.

4. **Consulting with Legal Counsel:**

   o **Seeking Legal Advice:**

      ▪ If the outcome of the investigation is unsatisfactory, consider seeking legal advice to explore your options:

         ▪ **Understanding Your Rights:** A lawyer can help clarify your rights, assess the merits of your case, and provide guidance on potential legal actions you might take.

         ▪ **Assessing the Feasibility of Legal Action:** If you feel your rights have been violated, legal counsel can help determine if pursuing a lawsuit is a viable option. They can also help navigate the complexities of employment law.

5. **Documenting Continued Issues:**

   o **Ongoing Documentation:**

      ▪ If you continue to experience discrimination or retaliation after the investigation, document each incident meticulously:

         ▪ **Detailed Records:** Keep detailed records of any further incidents of discrimination or retaliation, including dates, times, descriptions of events, and any witnesses present. This documentation can be vital for future complaints or legal action.

         ▪ **Communicate with HR Again:** Bring any ongoing issues to the attention of HR, highlighting that the resolution did not fully address your concerns. Be prepared to provide your documentation as evidence.

Conclusion

Understanding the potential outcomes of an investigation into workplace discrimination and knowing the steps to take if you are dissatisfied with the results can empower you as an employee. While the investigation process aims to provide fair resolutions, it is essential to advocate for yourself and ensure that your rights are protected. If the outcome does not meet your expectations, various avenues exist to seek further action, from requesting reviews and pursuing internal processes to consulting legal counsel. Your experience matters, and taking informed steps can contribute to fostering a more equitable workplace. Remember that standing up for your rights not only benefits you but also helps create a healthier work environment for all employees.

The next chapter will explain what retaliation is, how to recognize it, and what steps you can take if you face retaliation after reporting discrimination or asserting your rights in the workplace.

Chapter 7: Dealing with Retaliation

Retaliation occurs when an employer takes adverse action against an employee for asserting their rights, such as filing a discrimination complaint, participating in an investigation, or speaking out against unfair treatment. Retaliation is illegal, and if you experience it, it's important to document any incidents and report them to HR or seek legal advice. By understanding your rights and taking prompt action, you can protect yourself and ensure that your workplace remains free from retaliation.

7.1 Definition of Retaliation

1. **What Constitutes Retaliatory Actions:**

   o Retaliation occurs when an employer takes adverse action against an employee for engaging in protected activities, such as reporting discrimination, participating in investigations, or asserting their rights under employment laws. Key examples of retaliatory actions include:

      ▪ **Termination:** Firing an employee shortly after they file a complaint can be a clear indicator of retaliation, especially if the termination appears to be unrelated to job performance.

      ▪ **Demotion:** Reducing an employee's rank or responsibilities as a consequence of their complaint can signal retaliation, particularly if the demotion is sudden or unjustified.

      ▪ **Salary Reduction:** Decreasing an employee's pay following their report of discrimination can be a retaliatory act, especially if the pay cut occurs without a clear justification related to performance.

      ▪ **Harassment:** Subjecting the employee to hostile behavior, such as ridicule, bullying, or increased scrutiny after they report an issue, can create a toxic work environment and constitute retaliation.

      ▪ **Exclusion:** Isolating the employee from team activities or opportunities can serve as a form of punishment and can impact their professional development and morale.

2. **Real-Life Examples of Retaliation:**

  - **Case Study 1:** An employee files a complaint about sexual harassment by a supervisor. After the complaint, the employee is given a negative performance review that impacts their bonus, despite their performance being satisfactory prior to the report.

  - **Case Study 2:** A worker reports unsafe working conditions to management. Subsequently, they are reassigned to a less desirable shift, leading to a loss of hours and income, which can be viewed as a retaliatory measure.

  - **Case Study 3:** After raising concerns about racial discrimination in hiring practices, an employee finds themselves excluded from important meetings and team discussions, effectively sidelining them and diminishing their role within the organization.

7.2 Legal Protections Against Retaliation

1. **Overview of Laws Protecting Against Retaliation:**

  - Various federal and state laws offer robust protections against retaliation for employees who assert their rights. Key laws include:

    - **Title VII of the Civil Rights Act:** Prohibits retaliation against employees who oppose discriminatory practices or participate in investigations. This law applies to various forms of discrimination, including race, color, national origin, sex, and religion.

    - **Americans with Disabilities Act (ADA):** Protects individuals from retaliation for asserting their rights related to disability discrimination, including requests for reasonable accommodations.

    - **Age Discrimination in Employment Act (ADEA):** Shields older employees from retaliation after filing complaints regarding age discrimination, ensuring they can advocate for their rights without fear.

    - **Whistleblower Protection Act:** Offers protections for employees who report violations of laws or regulations, preventing adverse actions from employers in response to such reporting.

2. **How to File a Retaliation Claim:**

   o If you believe you have experienced retaliation, it is crucial to follow these steps:

     ▪ **Document Everything:** Maintain thorough records of the retaliatory actions you experience. This documentation should include specific incidents, dates, times, and descriptions of what occurred, providing a clear timeline of events.

     ▪ **File with the EEOC:** Submit a charge of discrimination to the Equal Employment Opportunity Commission (EEOC) or your local fair employment practices agency. Be mindful of the filing deadlines, which typically range from 180 to 300 days from the date of the retaliatory act.

     ▪ **Consult State Laws:** In addition to federal protections, review state-specific laws that may provide additional protections against retaliation or extend filing periods. Some states have more stringent laws than federal ones, offering broader definitions of retaliation.

7.3 Steps to Take if You Experience Retaliation

1. **Documenting Retaliatory Actions:**

   o Keeping meticulous documentation is essential for building a strong case against retaliation. Here are key practices:

     ▪ **Detailed Incident Reports:** Write clear, concise descriptions of each retaliatory action, including the context in which it occurred and the individuals involved. Ensure that your accounts are as objective as possible.

     ▪ **Collect Supporting Evidence:** Gather relevant documents such as emails, text messages, performance reviews, or any witness statements that can corroborate your experience of retaliation. These pieces of evidence can significantly strengthen your case.

- **Maintain a Timeline:** Create a timeline of events that connects your initial complaint or protected activity to the subsequent retaliatory actions. This visual representation can help illustrate a clear cause-and-effect relationship.

2. **Seeking Legal Counsel and Support:**

   o If you suspect you are facing retaliation, it is crucial to seek legal advice to understand your rights and options:

     - **Consult an Employment Lawyer:** An attorney specializing in employment law can evaluate your situation, advise you on the best course of action, and represent you if you decide to pursue legal action. A lawyer can also help you understand the nuances of your case and the relevant laws that apply.

     - **Contact Advocacy Organizations:** Reach out to local or national organizations that specialize in workers' rights or anti-discrimination efforts for support and guidance. These organizations may offer resources, legal advice, or connections to lawyers who can help.

     - **Utilize Employee Assistance Programs (EAPs):** If available, consider accessing your employer's EAP for confidential counseling and resources to help you cope with the emotional stress of retaliation. These programs can provide support and guidance in navigating workplace challenges.

Conclusion

Dealing with retaliation in the workplace is a daunting challenge, particularly after taking the courageous step of reporting discrimination or asserting your rights. Understanding what constitutes retaliation, knowing your legal protections, and taking proactive steps to document incidents and seek support are essential for navigating this difficult situation. By empowering yourself with knowledge about your rights and available resources, you can stand firm against retaliatory actions and foster a more equitable workplace.

Remember, retaliation is illegal, and you have the right to advocate for yourself without fear of adverse consequences. Your experience matters, and taking informed steps can contribute to a healthier work environment for all employees. Whether through documenting incidents, seeking legal counsel, or engaging with supportive organizations, know that you are not alone, and there are avenues available to protect your rights.

The next chapter walks you through the process of filing a complaint with a civil rights agency if your employer fails to properly address your discrimination report. You'll learn the necessary steps, key details to include, and how to ensure your complaint is properly handled.

Chapter 8: Filing Your Complaint

Filing a discrimination complaint is a pivotal step for employees who have experienced unfair treatment in the workplace. If an employee believes they have been discriminated against based on factors such as race, gender, disability, religion, or other protected characteristics, and their employer fails to properly address or resolve the issue, filing an external complaint may be necessary.

This chapter outlines the essential components of the employment discrimination complaint process, guiding individuals through the necessary steps to seek justice effectively. By understanding the types of discrimination, the specific processes for filing complaints with federal, state, and local agencies, and the resources available, employees can navigate the legal system with greater confidence and clarity.

If the employer does not take appropriate action to resolve the discrimination, the employee can file a complaint with external agencies like the Equal Employment Opportunity Commission (EEOC) or relevant state agencies. These external complaints provide a formal mechanism for employees to challenge discriminatory practices and seek legal remedies.

8.1 Understanding the Complaint Process

- **Importance of Filing:**

    - Filing a complaint serves multiple vital functions. It allows individuals to address personal grievances and seek justice while simultaneously fostering broader societal accountability. By formally documenting experiences of discrimination, Complainants contribute to a collective understanding of systemic issues, helping to identify patterns that necessitate change within organizations and communities.

- **Types of Complaints:**

    - There are generally two main pathways for filing a complaint: administrative complaints and civil lawsuits. Administrative complaints are typically filed with governmental agencies, such as the Equal Employment Opportunity Commission (EEOC). These complaints often lead to investigations and mediations aimed at resolving the issue. If these avenues do not yield satisfactory results, individuals may pursue civil lawsuits, where they can seek monetary damages or injunctive relief through the court system. This option allows for broader legal arguments and the potential for jury trials.

8.2 Federal Complaint Process

- **Equal Employment Opportunity Commission (EEOC):**

  o The EEOC is the primary federal agency for addressing discrimination in employment. Complainants can file a charge through various methods:

- **How to File:** Individuals can utilize the EEOC's user-friendly online portal, which guides users through the required information. Alternatively, they can file in person at local EEOC offices or submit a written complaint via mail.

  o **Eligibility:** Eligibility extends to current employees, former employees, and job applicants who believe they have been discriminated against based on protected characteristics. It's important to note the time limits: typically, individuals have 180 days from the date of the discriminatory act to file a charge, although some states offer longer periods.

- **Required Information:** When filing, Complainants should be prepared to provide personal information, a detailed description of the discriminatory behavior, and any supporting evidence, such as emails or witness statements.

8.3 State and Local Complaint Processes

- **State Agencies:**

  o Each state has its own human rights agency that addresses discrimination complaints. Individuals should familiarize themselves with state laws, which may offer protections beyond federal standards. Filing processes often mirror those of the EEOC, with options for online submissions or in-person visits.

- **Local Ordinances:**

  o Many cities and counties have local agencies that provide accessible complaint processes, often addressing issues not covered by state or federal laws. Researching local ordinances can reveal additional protections. Community organizations frequently offer support in navigating these processes, providing both guidance and emotional assistance.

8.4 Resources for Complainants

- **Guides and Templates:**

  o Numerous online resources offer filing guides that break down the complaint process step-by-step. Additionally, sample templates can help individuals structure their complaints effectively, ensuring that all relevant information is included.

- **Legal Aid:**

  o For those unable to afford legal representation, organizations like the American Civil Liberties Union (ACLU) and local legal aid societies can provide essential resources. Pro bono programs may also be available, offering free legal services for significant civil rights cases.

8.5 Preparing for the Complaint Process

- **Gathering Necessary Documents:**

  o Before filing a complaint, individuals should compile relevant documents to support their claims. This may include employment records, performance evaluations, communication related to the incident, and notes detailing discriminatory remarks or actions.

- **Emotional Preparation:**

- Filing a complaint can be an emotionally charged experience, often leading to stress or anxiety. Seeking support from friends, family, or mental health professionals can be beneficial, helping individuals cope with the challenges they may face during this process.

8.6 Understanding the Complaint Form

When filing a complaint, whether online, in person, or via mail, individuals will typically encounter a complaint form that requires specific information. Understanding what the form might ask can help prepare you for the process and ensure that your submission is complete and effective.

Typical Questions on the Complaint Form:

1. **Personal Information:**

   - Full name, address, phone number, and email.

   - Demographic information, such as age, gender, and race, to establish the basis for your claim.

2. **Details of the Discrimination:**

   - A clear and concise description of the discriminatory actions you experienced, including who was involved, what occurred, when it happened, and where it took place.

   - Identification of the specific protected characteristic(s) that were the basis of the discrimination (e.g., race, gender, disability).

3. **Supporting Evidence:**

   - Requests for any supporting documentation, such as emails, texts, photographs, performance evaluations, or witness statements that substantiate your claims.

4. **Desired Resolution:**

   - A section where you can specify what outcome you are seeking, such as monetary compensation, policy changes, or other forms of relief.

Seeking Assistance:

Filing a complaint can be a complex and sometimes overwhelming process. If you have questions or need help completing the form, don't hesitate to ask for assistance. Most agencies have staff members available to help you understand the form and ensure that your submission is as thorough as possible.

- **Language Assistance:** If English is not your first language, you can request a translator to help you complete the form. Many agencies provide translation services or can assist you in finding someone who can translate for you, ensuring that language barriers do not hinder your ability to file a complaint.

- **In-Person Help:** Visiting local offices allows for face-to-face assistance, where staff can guide you through the process, clarify any confusing sections of the form, and provide immediate answers to your questions.

Taking advantage of these resources can empower you to present a strong case and ensure that your voice is heard throughout the complaint process.

8.7 Common Issues to Avoid

- **Incomplete Information:**

  - Thoroughness is key when filing a complaint. Providing incomplete or vague details can lead to delays or dismissals. Taking the time to double-check submissions can prevent unnecessary complications.

- **Missed Deadlines:**

  - Keeping track of filing deadlines is crucial. Setting reminders and filing well in advance of the deadline can help avoid last-minute issues that may jeopardize the complaint.

- **Retaliation Concerns:**

  - Understanding protections against retaliation is vital for Complainants. Many laws protect individuals from adverse actions as a result of filing a complaint, empowering them to assert their rights without fear of further discrimination.

Conclusion

In summary, understanding the filing process for discrimination complaints is essential for anyone seeking justice. By familiarizing themselves with the necessary steps and utilizing available resources, individuals can effectively navigate the complexities of the legal system. Filing a complaint not only serves personal advocacy but also contributes to a broader culture that challenges discriminatory practices. It is imperative for individuals to take action against discrimination, standing up not only for themselves but for the collective rights of all who face injustice.

The next chapter walks you through the process of seeking legal help if your workplace rights are being violated, ensuring you know when and how to take the next step in protecting yourself.

Chapter 9: Seeking Legal Assistance

If you're facing discrimination at work and feel your rights are being violated, seeking legal assistance can help you understand your options and protect your interests. A lawyer specializing in employment law can provide guidance on whether you have a valid case, assist in filing complaints, and represent you in legal proceedings if necessary. It's important to consult with an attorney early on to ensure you're taking the right steps to address the situation effectively.

9.1 When to Consider Hiring an Attorney

1. **Indicators That Legal Assistance Is Necessary:**

    o **Severe or Ongoing Issues:**

      ▪ If you find yourself facing persistent discrimination, harassment, or retaliation that disrupts your work life, legal expertise can help clarify your rights. This is especially critical if the discrimination is systematic and affects multiple employees, as it may indicate a broader issue within the organization.

    o **Inadequate Employer Response:**

      ▪ When you report incidents of discrimination or harassment and your employer downplays your concerns or fails to take appropriate action, it's a sign that you may need legal assistance. An attorney can guide you through escalating the matter and provide clarity on your rights under the law.

    o **Complex Legal Issues:**

      ▪ If your situation involves multiple forms of discrimination (e.g., race and gender), nuances in employment law, or complicated workplace dynamics (like retaliation or hostile work environments), having a legal professional can help navigate these complexities.

    o **Desire for Formal Action:**

      ▪ If you're considering filing a complaint with the Equal Employment Opportunity Commission (EEOC) or pursuing a lawsuit, legal assistance is vital. An attorney can ensure you understand the necessary steps and timelines involved in these processes, increasing your chances of a successful outcome.

2. **Types of Lawyers to Consider:**

   o **Employment Law Specialists:**

     ▪ Look for attorneys who focus on employment law and have a track record in handling discrimination and retaliation cases. Their specialized knowledge can provide you with the best chance of navigating your situation effectively.

   o **Civil Rights Attorneys:**

     ▪ If your case involves broader civil rights violations, such as systemic discrimination, civil rights attorneys can help advocate for not just your individual case but also for changes within the organization or industry.

   o **Litigation vs. Mediation Attorneys:**

     ▪ Depending on your preferred method of resolution, choose attorneys experienced in either litigation or mediation. Each requires different strategies, and understanding your goals can guide your selection.

9.2 How to Choose the Right Lawyer

1. **Questions to Ask During Consultations:**

   o **Experience:**

     ▪ "How many similar cases have you handled, and what were the outcomes?" This question helps you gauge the attorney's familiarity with cases like yours.

   o **Approach:**

     ▪ "What is your strategy for handling cases like mine?" Understanding their methods can reveal whether they align with your expectations and style.

   o **Communication:**

- "How will we communicate throughout the process, and how often can I expect updates?" Clear and consistent communication is crucial for keeping you informed about your case's progress.

  o **Case Assessment:**

  - "Based on what I've shared, what do you think my chances of success are?" This can help you gauge their realistic view of your case and their confidence in your situation.

  o **Timeline:**

  - "What is the expected timeline for this process?" Knowing what to expect can help you prepare for the upcoming steps and manage your expectations.

2. **Understanding Fee Structures:**

   o **Contingency Fees:**

   - Many employment lawyers work on a contingency basis, meaning they only get paid if you win your case. Clarify what percentage they take from your recovery and any potential costs you may still be responsible for, such as filing fees or expert witness fees.

   o **Hourly Fees:**

   - Some attorneys charge by the hour. Be sure to inquire about their hourly rate, how they bill for their time, and any additional costs that may arise during your case. Understanding what is included in their hourly fee is essential.

   o **Retainers:**

   - If applicable, discuss any retainer fees that may be required upfront. Understand how these fees will be applied to your overall legal costs and what happens if you decide to terminate the attorney-client relationship.

9.3 The Legal Process

1. **Overview of Mediation, Arbitration, and Litigation:**

- o **Mediation:**
  - This is a voluntary process where a neutral third party helps both sides negotiate a resolution. Mediation is typically less formal than court proceedings and can often lead to quicker outcomes while maintaining confidentiality and preserving relationships.

- o **Arbitration:**
  - In arbitration, a neutral third party listens to both sides and makes a binding decision. This process can be faster than litigation and is often less formal, but it may limit your ability to appeal the arbitrator's decision and may be mandated by employment contracts.

- o **Litigation:**
  - This involves taking legal action in court, which can be lengthy and public. Litigation encompasses filing a complaint, engaging in discovery, going to trial, and potentially pursuing appeals. It usually requires more time and resources than mediation or arbitration, so understanding each step is crucial.

2. **Expected Timelines and Processes for Legal Action:**

- o **Initial Consultation:**
  - This typically occurs within a few weeks of reaching out to a lawyer. During this meeting, you can discuss your situation, understand your rights, and determine the best course of action moving forward.

- o **Filing a Complaint:**
  - If you decide to file a complaint with the EEOC or in court, the timeframe can vary. This step might take anywhere from weeks to several months, depending on the specifics of your case and the legal requirements involved.

- o **Discovery Phase:**

- If litigation is pursued, this phase can last several months to over a year, as both parties gather and exchange evidence. The discovery process is crucial for building a strong case, allowing both sides to assess the strengths and weaknesses of their positions.

  - o **Resolution:**

    - The time required for resolution can differ greatly depending on whether you choose mediation, arbitration, or litigation. Mediation often leads to quicker outcomes, while litigation can extend the timeline significantly, sometimes lasting years before reaching a resolution.

9.4 Resources for Finding Legal Aid and Support

1. **National and Local Legal Aid Organizations:**

   - o Numerous organizations provide legal assistance to those facing discrimination. Consider reaching out to:

     - **National Employment Lawyers Association (NELA):** This organization helps connect individuals with employment law specialists who focus on employee rights and workplace discrimination. Their website often includes resources and information on finding qualified attorneys.

     - **Legal Services Corporation (LSC):** A national nonprofit organization that funds legal aid organizations across the country, providing resources and referrals for low-income individuals in need of legal assistance.

     - **State Bar Associations:** Many state bar associations have lawyer referral services, helping you find attorneys who specialize in employment law within your locality. They may also provide resources for understanding your rights.

2. **Online Resources and Directories:**

   - o Utilize online platforms to research and connect with legal resources:

     - **Avvo:** This online directory allows you to search for lawyers based on practice area and location, along with reviews and ratings from previous clients, making it easier to find someone who fits your needs.

- **Justia:** Offers a comprehensive lawyer directory along with resources on various legal topics, helping you find attorneys specializing in employment law and discrimination.

- **LawHelp.org:** A valuable site for finding free legal aid resources in your state, including information about local organizations and their services. This resource can guide you to appropriate support based on your specific needs.

Conclusion

Understanding when and how to seek legal assistance is essential for effectively navigating workplace discrimination and retaliation. By knowing the indicators for hiring an attorney, how to choose the right legal representative, and what to expect during the legal process, you empower yourself to advocate for your rights. Additionally, leveraging resources for finding legal aid can provide you with the support necessary to achieve justice and resolution in your workplace issues. With the right guidance and information, you can take meaningful steps toward securing a fair and equitable work environment.

The next chapter explores strategies for creating a more inclusive workplace, providing actionable steps to foster diversity, respect, and equality for all employees.

Chapter 10: Building an Inclusive Workplace

Creating an inclusive workplace is essential not only for fostering a fair and respectful environment but also for enhancing organizational success. An inclusive culture values diversity and ensures that all employees, regardless of their background or identity, feel respected, supported, and empowered to thrive. This chapter will explore practical strategies for promoting inclusivity, addressing biases, and building a workplace where everyone feels they belong. By committing to inclusivity, employers can improve employee satisfaction, retention, and overall performance, while contributing to a more equitable and innovative workplace.

10.1 Tips for Employees on Fostering Inclusivity

1. **Engaging in Diversity Training Programs:**

   o **Participation in Training:** Actively participate in any diversity, equity, and inclusion (DEI) training programs offered by your organization. These sessions are designed to enhance your understanding of different perspectives and equip you with tools to engage effectively with colleagues from diverse backgrounds.

   o **Sharing Knowledge:** After attending training, consider sharing key insights and learnings with your team or department. Hosting informal discussions or creating a summary document can reinforce your knowledge while encouraging others to think critically about inclusivity.

   o **Continuous Learning:** Seek out additional resources, such as workshops, webinars, and books on diversity and inclusion. Staying informed about best practices helps you bring fresh ideas to the workplace and fosters a culture of continuous improvement.

2. **Advocating for Policy Changes Within the Organization:**

   o **Identify Areas for Improvement:** Assess existing policies and practices that may inadvertently foster exclusion. Collect data and feedback from colleagues to identify specific areas where change is needed, such as recruitment strategies, promotion criteria, and workplace accommodations.

- Propose Solutions: Develop well-researched proposals for policy changes that can enhance inclusivity. This might involve suggesting more inclusive hiring practices, implementing mentorship programs for underrepresented groups, or revising policies related to flexible work arrangements.

- Engagement with Leadership: Prepare a presentation or report to share your findings with leadership or human resources. Emphasize the business case for inclusivity, highlighting how diverse teams drive innovation and improve company performance.

10.2 Strategies for Advocating for Diversity and Inclusion

1. **Creating Employee Resource Groups (ERGs):**

    - **Formation of ERGs:** Encourage the establishment of employee resource groups that represent various demographics, such as race, gender, sexual orientation, and disability. These groups provide a platform for employees to connect, share experiences, and advocate for their needs within the organization.

    - **Support and Resources:** Work with management to secure resources for these groups, including budgets for events, meeting spaces, and access to company communications. Highlight how ERGs contribute to employee morale and retention, and advocate for their integration into the organizational structure.

    - **Showcasing Achievements:** Promote the accomplishments and initiatives of ERGs to the wider organization. This visibility can help garner support for diversity efforts and demonstrate the value of these groups in enhancing workplace culture.

2. **Building Coalitions with Like-Minded Colleagues:**

    - **Collaborative Advocacy:** Connect with colleagues who share your commitment to diversity and inclusion. Together, you can amplify your voices and push for meaningful changes within the organization. Regular meetings can help coordinate efforts and maintain momentum.

    - **Organizing Initiatives:** Collaborate on initiatives such as awareness campaigns, workshops, or community service projects that promote inclusivity. This not only raises awareness but also strengthens relationships among employees and creates a sense of shared purpose.

- ○ **Leveraging Influence:** Utilize the collective influence of your coalition to advocate for diversity-related initiatives with management. Emphasize the positive impact these efforts can have on workplace culture, employee engagement, and overall productivity.

10.3 The Role of Bystanders in Combating Discrimination

1. **How to Intervene Safely and Effectively:**

   - ○ **Recognizing Discriminatory Behavior:** Learn to identify instances of discrimination or harassment in the workplace, including both overt acts and subtle microaggressions. Being aware allows you to respond appropriately and help create a safer work environment.

   - ○ **Assessing the Situation:** Before intervening, evaluate the context of the situation. Consider your own safety, the safety of others, and the potential impact of your intervention. Sometimes, a quiet approach or discreet report to HR may be more effective than direct confrontation.

   - ○ **Choosing Your Approach:** Decide how to intervene—whether through direct confrontation, offering support to the affected individual, or reporting the behavior to management or HR. Each situation may require a different approach, so consider the best course of action based on the circumstances.

2. **Encouraging a Culture of Accountability:**

   - ○ **Modeling Inclusive Behavior:** Set an example for your colleagues by consistently demonstrating inclusive behavior. Your actions can inspire others to follow suit, contributing to a workplace culture that values diversity and respect.

   - ○ **Creating Safe Spaces for Discussion:** Advocate for regular discussions about inclusivity and discrimination in team meetings. Encourage open dialogue where employees feel comfortable sharing their experiences and concerns, fostering a sense of community and support.

- ○ **Promoting Reporting Mechanisms:** Ensure that there are accessible and effective channels for reporting discrimination or harassment. Encourage colleagues to utilize these mechanisms, reinforcing that accountability is a shared responsibility and that everyone plays a role in fostering a respectful workplace.

Conclusion

Fostering an inclusive workplace is a shared responsibility that requires active participation from all employees. By engaging in diversity training, advocating for policy changes, creating employee resource groups, and intervening when witnessing discrimination, employees can collectively contribute to a more equitable work environment. Building a culture of accountability and support not only enhances the workplace experience for everyone but also strengthens the organization's overall performance. With these strategies, employees can empower themselves and their colleagues to create lasting change in their workplace culture, ensuring that diversity and inclusion are not just goals, but integral values that guide everyday interactions and decision-making.

The next chapter focuses on how to support your colleagues in the face of workplace discrimination and actively contribute to fostering an inclusive, equitable environment for everyone.

Chapter 11: Supporting Your Colleagues

Supporting your colleagues is an essential aspect of fostering a positive, inclusive workplace culture. Whether it's standing up against discrimination, offering emotional support during difficult times, or advocating for equal treatment, each employee has the power to create a more respectful and collaborative environment. This chapter explores how you can support your coworkers, particularly those who may be facing discrimination or marginalization, and the importance of allyship in driving positive change. By actively supporting one another, employees can not only help address individual challenges but also contribute to a culture of fairness, trust, and mutual respect that benefits everyone in the organization.

11.1 How to Be an Ally to Colleagues Facing Discrimination

1. **Recognizing and Validating Their Experiences:**

   o **Active Listening:**

     ▪ **Focus on the Speaker:** When a colleague shares their experience, give them your full attention. This means putting away distractions, making eye contact, and using body language that shows you're engaged.

     ▪ **Empathetic Responses:** Use phrases like "That sounds really difficult" or "I can't imagine how challenging that must be for you" to convey empathy. This validation can help your colleague feel understood and supported.

     ▪ **Encouraging Open Dialogue:** Create an environment where colleagues feel safe sharing their experiences. Let them know that you're available to listen whenever they need to talk.

2. **Speaking Up Against Discrimination and Supporting Actions:**

   o **Confronting Discriminatory Behavior:**

     ▪ **Immediate Intervention:** If you witness discriminatory comments or actions in real time, calmly address them on the spot. For example, you might say, "I don't think that's an appropriate way to speak about someone."

- **Private Conversations:** After the fact, consider having a private conversation with the person who made the comment. Share how their words may have affected others and suggest alternative approaches to communication.

- **Encouraging Collective Action:**

  - **Forming Alliances:** Join forces with other allies to create a unified front against discrimination. This collective voice can amplify your efforts and encourage more people to take a stand.

  - **Promoting Initiatives:** Advocate for workplace initiatives aimed at diversity and inclusion, such as diversity committees or events that celebrate various cultures and identities. Your participation shows solidarity and encourages others to join.

- **Being Visible in Your Support:**

  - **Attend and Support Events:** Show your support by attending diversity and inclusion events, whether they are formal trainings, community outreach programs, or awareness campaigns.

  - **Using Social Media:** Leverage social media platforms to share resources, support movements, or highlight the achievements of underrepresented groups within your organization.

11.2 Recognizing and Addressing Microaggressions

1. **Understanding What Microaggressions Are:**

   - **Definition and Impact:** Microaggressions are often subtle, unintentional comments or actions that convey a negative message or stereotype about a marginalized group. They can accumulate over time, leading to a hostile work environment for those targeted.

   - **Examples:** Recognize common phrases or actions that may be considered microaggressions, such as comments implying someone is not "typical" for their race or questioning a woman's competence based on her appearance.

2. **Strategies for Addressing Microaggressions in the Workplace:**

- Speaking Up:

  - **Use "I" Statements:** When addressing a microaggression, frame your response with "I" statements to express how the comment made you feel. For instance, "I felt uncomfortable when I heard that comment because it reinforces a stereotype."

  - **Follow-Up Conversations:** Encourage an ongoing dialogue by asking the individual if they would be open to discussing the impact of their words. This can lead to greater awareness and change.

- **Educating Others:**

  - **Resource Sharing:** Provide resources—articles, videos, or training materials—that explain microaggressions and their effects. This helps cultivate understanding and awareness among colleagues.

  - **Facilitating Workshops:** If appropriate, propose workshops or training sessions focused on recognizing and addressing microaggressions. Encourage participation from all levels of the organization.

- **Creating a Safe Environment:**

  - **Establishing Norms:** Work with management to establish norms for communication that promote respect and inclusivity. This could include guidelines for meetings that emphasize respectful dialogue and discourage dismissive language.

  - **Encouraging Reporting:** Make it clear that microaggressions can and should be reported. Provide clear channels for reporting incidents, ensuring employees feel supported in doing so.

11.3 Creating Support Networks

1. **Building Peer Support Groups:**

   - **Establishing Safe Spaces:**

- **Regular Meetings:** Organize regular meetings for support groups where employees can share experiences and discuss challenges related to discrimination. Create a structured format to encourage participation, such as facilitated discussions or themed topics.

- **Encouraging Diverse Participation:** Invite employees from different backgrounds to participate, ensuring a rich diversity of experiences and perspectives within the group. This fosters a deeper understanding of the complexities of discrimination.

- **Promoting Inclusivity:**

    - **Open Membership:** Ensure these support groups are inclusive and accessible to all employees. Highlight the importance of allyship and encourage allies to join to better understand the challenges faced by their colleagues.

    - **Networking Opportunities:** Use support group meetings to create networking opportunities that connect employees across different departments and levels within the organization.

2. **Resources for Mentoring and Peer Advocacy:**

    - **Mentorship Programs:**

        - **Structured Mentorship:** Advocate for the development of structured mentorship programs where individuals from marginalized backgrounds can be paired with experienced mentors who can offer guidance and support in their career development.

        - **Highlighting Success Stories:** Share success stories from mentorship relationships within the organization to encourage participation and demonstrate the program's value.

    - **Peer Advocacy Initiatives:**

        - **Supportive Action Plans:** Develop action plans that detail how peers can advocate for one another in meetings, during performance reviews, or when addressing workplace issues.

This structured support can help amplify voices that may otherwise go unheard.

- **Resource Sharing:** Create a repository of resources for employees to access when advocating for themselves or their colleagues, including templates for writing advocacy letters or strategies for presenting concerns to management.

Conclusion

Supporting colleagues who face discrimination is a crucial aspect of cultivating an inclusive workplace culture. By recognizing and validating their experiences, actively speaking out against discrimination, and creating supportive networks, employees can foster an environment where everyone feels valued and respected. Addressing microaggressions and promoting open dialogue about diversity and inclusion are essential steps in building a supportive workplace. Ultimately, by working together as allies, employees can create a culture of solidarity and accountability that benefits everyone and contributes to a more equitable workplace for all.

In the next and final chapter, we'll explore strategies for developing a mindset of resilience, including how to stand firm in the face of discrimination, manage stress effectively, and build emotional strength. By fostering a resilient mindset, you can better navigate workplace challenges, advocate for your rights, and emerge stronger from any adversity you face.

Chapter 12: Personal Empowerment and Resilience

Personal empowerment and resilience are key to navigating the challenges that may arise in the workplace, especially when faced with discrimination or adversity. This chapter focuses on building the inner strength to advocate for yourself, maintain your well-being, and bounce back from setbacks. By developing self-confidence, emotional intelligence, and coping strategies, you can take control of your career journey, protect your mental health, and thrive in environments that may not always be supportive. Empowering yourself not only helps you stand firm in your rights but also inspires others to do the same, creating a ripple effect that can lead to lasting positive change in the workplace.

12.1 Coping with the Emotional Impact of Discrimination

1. **Strategies for Self-Care and Mental Health:**

    o **Prioritizing Self-Care:**

        - **Physical Well-Being:** Engage in regular physical activity that you enjoy, such as walking, jogging, or joining a fitness class. Consistent exercise can reduce stress levels and enhance mood. Aim for at least 30 minutes of activity most days of the week.

        - **Nutrition and Sleep:** Maintain a balanced diet rich in fruits, vegetables, whole grains, and lean proteins. Proper nutrition supports both physical and mental health. Establish a regular sleep routine, aiming for 7-9 hours of quality sleep each night to help your body recover from stress.

    o **Mindfulness and Relaxation Techniques:**

        - **Meditation and Breathing Exercises:** Explore guided meditation apps or videos to help cultivate mindfulness. Breathing exercises, such as the 4-7-8 technique, can quickly reduce anxiety and promote a sense of calm.

        - **Yoga and Stretching:** Incorporate yoga or stretching into your routine to relieve physical tension and promote relaxation.

Even a few minutes of stretching can be beneficial during a work break.

- o **Finding Outlets for Expression:**

  - **Journaling:** Write regularly about your feelings, experiences, and reflections. This practice can help you process emotions and gain clarity on your experiences. Consider prompts that encourage reflection on your strengths and achievements.

  - **Creative Outlets:** Explore activities such as painting, writing poetry, or playing a musical instrument. Engaging in creative expression can provide an emotional release and foster resilience.

2. **Resources for Counseling and Support:**

- o **Therapy and Counseling Services:**

  - **Finding a Professional:** Research local therapists who specialize in workplace issues, discrimination, or trauma. Check online directories and read reviews to find a suitable match. Don't hesitate to reach out for initial consultations to gauge compatibility.

  - **Online Therapy Options:** Consider online platforms that offer therapy, such as BetterHelp or Talkspace, which can provide flexibility in scheduling and access to licensed professionals.

- o **Support Groups:**

  - **Peer Support Networks:** Seek out local or online support groups focused on workplace discrimination. Sharing experiences with peers can provide validation and help reduce feelings of isolation.

  - **Community Resources:** Investigate local organizations that focus on advocacy and support for marginalized groups, as they often offer workshops, counseling, and resources for empowerment.

12.2 Building Confidence to Stand Up for Your Rights

1. **Practical Exercises and Affirmations:**

- o **Developing Assertiveness:**
    - **Assertiveness Training:** Look for workshops or online courses that teach assertiveness skills. Learning how to express your needs clearly and respectfully can empower you to address discrimination effectively.
    - **Daily Affirmations:** Create a personalized list of affirmations that resonate with you. Phrases like "I deserve to be treated with respect" or "My voice matters" can reinforce your self-worth. Consider writing these affirmations on sticky notes and placing them in visible areas.
- o **Visualization Techniques:**
    - **Imagining Success:** Visualize yourself in a scenario where you successfully advocate for your rights. Picture the setting, the conversations, and the positive outcome. This mental rehearsal can build confidence and reduce anxiety.
    - **Role Models:** Identify individuals who inspire you—whether public figures, mentors, or colleagues—who have successfully navigated discrimination. Reflect on their qualities and how you can embody similar strengths.

2. **Role-Playing Scenarios for Difficult Conversations:**
    - o **Practicing Conversations:**
        - **Peer Role-Playing:** Partner with a trusted friend or colleague to practice handling conversations about discrimination. Focus on articulating your feelings and asserting your rights. This rehearsal can help you feel more prepared and less anxious in real situations.
        - **Feedback and Reflection:** After each role-play, discuss what went well and what could be improved. Constructive feedback can refine your communication skills and boost your confidence.
    - o **Scenario Preparation:**
        - **Common Situations:** Compile a list of common workplace scenarios where you might encounter discrimination or bias,

such as performance reviews or team meetings. Prepare responses for each, allowing you to feel more equipped to handle these situations when they arise.

- **Adaptive Strategies:** Develop multiple approaches for addressing difficult conversations, giving you the flexibility to adapt your response based on the situation and the person involved.

12.3 Resources for Further Support

1. **Employee Assistance Programs (EAPs):**

   o **Understanding EAPs:**

     - **What They Offer:** Many employers provide EAPs that offer free and confidential counseling services, legal assistance, and resources for personal and professional challenges. These programs can be a valuable resource during times of stress or conflict.

     - **How to Access:** Familiarize yourself with your workplace's EAP by reviewing employee handbooks or reaching out to HR for details on available services and how to access them.

   o **Utilizing EAPs Effectively:**

     - **Scheduling Appointments:** Don't hesitate to reach out for support when needed. Make appointments for counseling, workshops, or other available resources through your EAP. Remember, seeking help is a strength, not a weakness.

     - **Family Benefits:** Inquire if EAP services extend to family members. Many programs offer support for loved ones, which can be especially beneficial during challenging times.

2. **National Organizations and Hotlines for Support:**

   o **Key Resources:**

     - **National Women's Law Center:** Provides information on legal rights related to gender discrimination, including resources for filing complaints and seeking support.

- **Equal Employment Opportunity Commission (EEOC):** Offers guidance on filing discrimination complaints, understanding your rights, and accessing mediation services.

- **Hotlines for Immediate Support:** Familiarize yourself with hotlines such as the National Domestic Violence Hotline (1-800-799-SAFE) or the National Suicide Prevention Lifeline (1-800-273-TALK) for immediate assistance in crisis situations.

- **Advocacy Organizations:**

  - **Local Advocacy Groups:** Research local organizations dedicated to fighting workplace discrimination and promoting equality. Many offer workshops, resources, and community support that can be invaluable.

  - **Legal Aid Organizations:** Connect with organizations that provide legal assistance and advice related to workplace discrimination. Many have free or low-cost services available to help individuals navigate their rights.

Conclusion

Personal empowerment and resilience are essential components of navigating the challenges of workplace discrimination. By adopting self-care strategies, seeking support, and building confidence in standing up for your rights, you can cultivate a sense of agency in your professional life. Remember, you are not alone in this journey; numerous resources and communities are available to support you as you advocate for yourself and others. Empower yourself with knowledge and connection, and embrace the resilience that comes from standing up against discrimination.

Recap of Key Points

1. **The Importance of Understanding and Advocating for Your Rights:**

   - Throughout this guide, we've delved into the complexities of workplace discrimination, emphasizing the critical nature of understanding both your legal rights and the social dynamics at play. Knowledge empowers employees to recognize injustices and assert their rights effectively. Advocacy is not merely an individual pursuit; it fosters a supportive environment where everyone feels valued and respected. Understanding your rights can serve as a catalyst for change within your organization, encouraging a culture of accountability and respect.

2. **Encouragement to Take Proactive Steps Against Discrimination:**
   - We've outlined a range of practical strategies that can be employed when faced with discrimination. From documenting incidents meticulously to understanding the reporting mechanisms available within your organization, taking proactive measures is vital. Encouragingly, every small step can contribute to larger systemic changes. By speaking out, supporting colleagues, and engaging in constructive dialogue, you help create an atmosphere where discrimination is challenged and addressed. The power of collective action can amplify individual voices, leading to significant organizational change.

Encouragement to Stay Informed

1. **The Necessity of Ongoing Education About Workplace Rights:**
   - The legal landscape surrounding workplace discrimination is not static; it evolves with new legislation, court rulings, and societal shifts. Therefore, ongoing education is crucial. Engage with professional development opportunities such as workshops, webinars, and conferences focused on workplace rights and diversity issues. Subscribing to relevant newsletters and joining professional organizations can keep you informed about the latest developments. Additionally, fostering a culture of continuous learning within your workplace can help create an environment where everyone feels empowered to advocate for their rights.

2. **Commitment to Fostering a More Inclusive Work Environment:**
   - Building an inclusive workplace requires dedication and effort from everyone involved. It involves not only recognizing and addressing discriminatory practices but also celebrating diversity and promoting inclusivity actively. Encourage open conversations about diversity and inclusion, participate in employee resource groups, and advocate for policies that prioritize equity. Your commitment to fostering inclusivity can create a ripple effect, inspiring others to engage in similar initiatives, thereby enhancing the overall workplace culture.

Call to Action

1. **Empowering Readers to Advocate for Themselves and Their Colleagues:**

   o As you finish this guide, reflect on the power you hold as an individual within your workplace. The knowledge and strategies you've acquired are tools for advocacy—tools that can drive meaningful change. Stand firm in your rights and encourage your colleagues to do the same. By actively participating in discussions about discrimination and inclusivity, you contribute to a collective push for justice. Your actions, whether through speaking up against injustice or supporting anti-discrimination initiatives, are essential in fostering a respectful workplace.

2. **Join the Movement for Equality:**

   o Embrace your role as an advocate for equality in the workplace. Share your insights and experiences with others, engage in community discussions, and participate in movements that support workers' rights. The fight against discrimination is ongoing, and every individual's contribution is vital. By taking action—whether it's initiating conversations, supporting policy changes, or educating yourself and others—you can be a part of a larger movement toward equity and inclusion. Together, we can create workplaces where everyone feels safe, respected, and empowered to thrive. Let your voice echo in the call for change, and take the necessary steps to champion equality, not just for yourself but for all.

In conclusion, this book is not just a resource—it's a call to action. Discrimination, in any form, has no place in the modern workplace, and armed with the knowledge contained in this guide, you are empowered to recognize, confront, and challenge it.

By understanding your legal rights, knowing how to identify discriminatory behavior, and learning the steps to take when discrimination occurs, you can navigate the complexities of workplace laws with confidence and clarity. Whether you're facing discrimination yourself or advocating for a more inclusive and equitable work environment, this book gives you the knowledge and tools to stand up for yourself and demand the respect and fairness you deserve.

The fight for workplace equality is ongoing, but with the right knowledge and a proactive approach, you can contribute to a culture of justice, respect, and opportunity for all. Your rights matter—get to know them, learn how to protect them, and, if and when necessary, take the steps to successfully defend them.

Appendices

Glossary of Key Terms

- **Accommodation**: Adjustments or modifications made in the workplace to enable individuals with disabilities to perform their job functions effectively. This can include changes to work schedules, alterations to physical spaces, or the provision of assistive technology.

- **Affirmative Action**: Policies and practices aimed at increasing opportunities for historically underrepresented groups in hiring, promotions, and other employment decisions. These measures are designed to correct past discrimination and foster diversity in the workplace.

- **At-Will Employment**: A type of employment relationship where either the employer or employee can terminate the relationship at any time, with or without cause, as long as the termination doesn't violate any laws (e.g., discrimination laws).

- **Claim**: A formal assertion made by an individual alleging discrimination or unfair treatment in the workplace. This can involve filing a complaint with an employer, agency, or court to seek redress for perceived violations of rights.

- **Confidentiality**: The ethical and legal obligation to protect sensitive information related to discrimination complaints. This includes ensuring that the identities of complainants and the details of their cases are kept private during investigations.

- **Civil Rights**: Rights that protect individuals from unfair treatment based on characteristics such as race, gender, religion, national origin, and disability. In the workplace, these rights safeguard employees from discrimination and ensure equality of opportunity.

- **Discrimination**: Unjust or prejudicial treatment of an individual or group based on characteristics such as race, color, religion, sex, national origin, age, disability, or sexual orientation. Discrimination can occur in hiring, promotions, job assignments, and other employment practices.

- **Disparate Impact**: A legal theory used in discrimination cases where a seemingly neutral policy disproportionately affects members of a protected class, regardless of the intent behind the policy. This can occur even if the policy is applied uniformly.

- **Disparate Treatment**: A form of discrimination where individuals in similar situations are treated differently based on their protected characteristics. This can involve overt discrimination, such as biased comments or actions, as well as more subtle forms of unequal treatment.

- **Disability Discrimination**: Discrimination against an individual because of their physical or mental disabilities. Under the Americans with Disabilities Act (ADA), employers are required to provide reasonable accommodations to employees with disabilities.

- **EEOC (Equal Employment Opportunity Commission)**: The federal agency responsible for enforcing laws against workplace discrimination. The EEOC investigates complaints, mediates disputes, and can file lawsuits to protect individuals' rights.

- **Equal Pay Act**: A federal law enacted to abolish wage disparity based on sex. It mandates that men and women be paid equally for performing the same job, barring any legitimate differences in pay based on seniority, merit, or other factors.

- **Employment Discrimination**: The unfair or unequal treatment of employees based on their protected characteristics, such as race, gender, age, disability, or other attributes covered by anti-discrimination laws.

- **Employment Retirement Income Security Act (ERISA)**: A federal law that sets minimum standards for pension and health plans in private industry to protect employees' benefits.

- **Family and Medical Leave Act (FMLA)**: A U.S. federal law that allows eligible employees to take up to 12 weeks of unpaid leave per year for certain family and medical reasons, without losing their job or health benefits. The law also prohibits retaliation against employees who take FMLA leave.

- **Fair Labor Standards Act (FLSA)**: A federal law that establishes minimum wage, overtime pay, and child labor protections for workers. It is designed to ensure fair wages and working conditions across all industries.

- **Harassment**: A form of discrimination that involves unwelcome and offensive conduct that creates a hostile or intimidating work environment. Harassment can be based on various characteristics, including race, sex, age, and disability, and can take many forms, including verbal, physical, and visual conduct.

- **Hostile Work Environment**: A work environment where discriminatory conduct (e.g., harassment, offensive comments, or unfair treatment) creates an intimidating, uncomfortable, or abusive atmosphere, making it difficult for employees to perform their duties.

- **Microaggressions**: Subtle, often unintentional, comments or actions that convey derogatory or dismissive messages to individuals based on their marginalized identities. These can accumulate over time and contribute to a hostile work environment.

- **Mediation**: A voluntary process where a neutral third party helps resolve disputes between an employer and an employee, or between employees. Mediation aims to find a mutually acceptable solution without resorting to formal litigation.

- **Mandatory Arbitration**: A process where disputes, including discrimination claims, are resolved outside the courtroom by a neutral third party. Employees may be required to arbitrate claims rather than litigate them in court, which can limit their rights in certain cases.

- **Protected Class**: A group of individuals identified by specific characteristics that are legally protected from discrimination. This includes, but is not limited to, race, sex, age, religion, disability, and national origin.

- **Retaliation**: Any adverse action taken against an individual as a response to their participation in protected activities, such as reporting discrimination or participating in an investigation. Retaliation is illegal under various employment laws.

- **Reasonable Accommodation**: Modifications or adjustments to a job, work environment, or workplace policy that enable a qualified employee with a disability to perform their essential job functions. Employers are required to provide reasonable accommodations unless doing so would cause undue hardship.

- **Sex Discrimination**: Unfair treatment of an individual based on their sex, encompassing a wide range of issues, including gender identity, gender expression, and sexual orientation. This can manifest in hiring practices, promotions, pay disparities, and workplace treatment.

- **Sexual Harassment**: Unwelcome or inappropriate conduct of a sexual nature that creates a hostile or intimidating work environment. This includes verbal, physical, or visual behavior that interferes with an individual's ability to perform their job.

- **Sexual Orientation**: Refers to an individual's emotional, romantic, or sexual attraction to people of the same or different genders. Discrimination based on sexual orientation is increasingly recognized in legal frameworks as a form of discrimination.

- **Social Identity**: The way individuals define themselves in relation to the groups to which they belong, such as gender, race, ethnicity, religion, and sexual orientation. These identities can play a significant role in experiences of discrimination or privilege in the workplace.

- **Title VII of the Civil Rights Act**: A landmark federal law that prohibits employment discrimination based on race, color, religion, sex, or national origin. Title VII is foundational in the fight for civil rights in the workplace and provides mechanisms for individuals to seek justice against discriminatory practices.

- **Transparent Pay**: A practice where companies openly share salary data and pay structures, often as a way to reduce gender and racial pay gaps and ensure fair compensation for all employees.

- **Title I of the Americans with Disabilities Act (ADA)**: The section of the ADA that prohibits discrimination against qualified individuals with disabilities in all areas of public life, including employment. It also requires employers to provide reasonable accommodations for employees with disabilities.

- **The Pregnancy Discrimination Act**: An amendment to Title VII of the Civil Rights Act that prohibits discrimination based on pregnancy, childbirth, or related medical conditions. It mandates that women affected by pregnancy or related conditions must be treated the same as other employees with similar abilities or limitations.

- **Whistleblower**: An employee who exposes wrongdoing or illegal activities within their organization. Whistleblowers may face retaliation for their actions, and many laws exist to protect them from adverse consequences for reporting such behavior.

- **Workplace Equity**: The practice of ensuring all employees have access to the same opportunities, resources, and rewards, regardless of their background, identity, or circumstances. This includes addressing biases, pay disparities, and creating fair policies for all workers.

- **Workplace Diversity**: A commitment to creating a workforce that reflects a wide range of demographic characteristics, including race, gender, age, disability, and sexual orientation. Diversity initiatives aim to foster inclusivity and enrich the work environment.

- **Worker Adjustment and Retraining Notification (WARN) Act**: A U.S. federal law that requires employers to provide advance notice of mass layoffs or plant closures to affected employees. This law is designed to give workers time to prepare for job loss and seek alternative employment.

This glossary serves as a comprehensive reference for understanding key terms related to workplace discrimination and relevant federal legislation. By familiarizing yourself with these definitions, you can better navigate the legal landscape, advocate for your rights, and contribute to a more inclusive and equitable workplace.

Sample Forms for Reporting Discrimination

This section provides templates and examples of various forms that can be used to document incidents of discrimination and submit formal complaints. These sample forms can help employees articulate their experiences clearly and effectively, ensuring that all necessary information is captured for potential investigations.

1. Incident Report Form

[Your Name]
[Your Job Title]
[Date]
[Department/Team]
[Supervisor's Name]

Incident Date:
Time:
Location:

Describe the Incident: (Provide a detailed account of what happened, including who was involved, what was said or done, and the impact on you or others.)

Witnesses: (List any witnesses who observed the incident, including their names and contact information.)

Actions Taken: (Describe any actions you took in response to the incident, including discussions with HR or management.)

Desired Outcome: (Explain what resolution you seek from this report.)

Signature:
Date:

---

2. Formal Complaint Form to HR/Management

[Your Name]

[Your Job Title]
[Date]
[Department/Team]

To:
[HR/Manager's Name]
[Company Name]

Subject: Formal Complaint of Discrimination

I am writing to formally report an incident of discrimination that I have experienced at work. Below are the details of the incident:

1. Description of the Incident: (Provide a concise description of the incident, including dates, times, and specific actions that constitute discrimination.)

2. Basis of Discrimination: (Indicate the protected characteristic(s) that apply: race, gender, age, disability, etc.)

3. Impact of the Incident: (Explain how the incident has affected you personally or professionally.)

4. Previous Discussions: (Detail any prior discussions with HR or management regarding this matter and their responses.)

5. Requested Resolution: (Outline what you hope to achieve as a result of this complaint.)

Thank you for your attention to this matter. I look forward to your prompt response.

Sincerely,
[Your Signature]
[Your Contact Information]

3. Retaliation Reporting Form

[Your Name]
[Your Job Title]
[Date]
[Department/Team]

To:
[HR/Manager's Name]
[Company Name]

Subject: Report of Retaliation

I am writing to report retaliatory actions that I have experienced following my previous complaint about discrimination. Below are the details:

1. Date of Original Complaint:

_____

2. Description of Retaliation: (Detail the retaliatory actions taken against you, including dates and involved parties.)

_____

3. Impact of Retaliation: (Explain how these actions have affected you and your work environment.)

_____

4. Previous Discussions: (Include any discussions you've had with HR or management about this retaliation.)

_____

5. Requested Action: (What resolution are you seeking regarding the retaliatory actions?)

_____

Thank you for addressing this serious matter.

Sincerely,
[Your Signature]
[Your Contact Information]

_____

These sample forms serve as templates that employees can adapt to their specific situations when reporting discrimination or retaliation. Utilizing structured documentation helps ensure that all relevant details are included, facilitating a thorough investigation and appropriate response from management or HR.

Self-Assessment Tools

Here are some examples of self-assessment tools that can help evaluate your experiences and spot potential discrimination:

1. Incident Documentation Checklist

- **Date & Time**: When did the incident occur?

- **Location**: Where did the incident take place (e.g., office, meeting room, etc.)?

- **People Involved**: Who was involved in the incident (e.g., supervisor, colleague, HR representative)?

- **Nature of the Incident**: What happened? Describe the event in detail.

- **Your Response**: How did you respond at the time?

- **Witnesses**: Were there any witnesses? If so, who?

- **Impact**: How did the incident affect your work or emotional well-being?

2. Discrimination Pattern Tracker

- **Type of Discrimination**: What category does the behavior fall under? (e.g., race, gender, age, disability, etc.)

- **Frequency**: How often does this behavior occur? (e.g., once, weekly, occasionally)

- **Consistency**: Is the behavior directed only at you, or is it consistent across different individuals or situations?

- **Severity**: How severe is the impact? Does it affect your job performance, career progression, or mental health?

- **Response from Management**: How has your employer responded (if at all)? Have you raised the issue, and if so, what was the outcome?

3. Reflection Questions

- **Do I feel that I am being treated fairly compared to my colleagues?**
  (Consider factors like workload, opportunities, respect, and recognition.)

- **Have I been subjected to any comments or actions that seem biased or offensive?**
  (Examples: jokes, assumptions about your abilities, exclusion from opportunities based on your protected characteristics.)

- **Have I been denied opportunities or privileges that are typically available to others?**
  (Examples: promotions, raises, training, access to important projects.)

- **Have I experienced any retaliation after reporting concerns or complaints?**
  (Examples: negative performance reviews, isolation, change in job duties.)

- **How would I describe the work environment?**
  (Consider factors like inclusivity, respect, diversity, and whether you feel supported.)

4. Impact Reflection Tool

- **Work Performance**: How has the situation affected your ability to perform your job duties?

- **Emotional Impact**: How do you feel when you encounter these issues (e.g., anxious, frustrated, isolated)?

- **Physical Impact**: Has the situation caused physical symptoms (e.g., stress-related illness, sleep disturbances)?

- **Career Progression**: Has the issue affected your opportunities for promotion, pay raises, or professional development?

- **Work Relationships**: How has the situation impacted your relationships with colleagues, supervisors, or subordinates?

5. Action Plan for Next Steps

- **What is the best course of action to address this situation?**
  (Examples: reporting to HR, seeking legal advice, documenting incidents, speaking to a mentor.)

- **What is my desired outcome?**
  (Examples: resolution through HR, policy change, awareness training, or pursuing legal action.)

- **What evidence do I need to gather?**
  (Examples: emails, performance reviews, witness statements, written notes of incidents.)

- **Who can I talk to for support?**
  (Examples: trusted colleagues, HR representatives, family members, legal professionals.)

These self-assessment tools can help you identify patterns of discrimination, document key incidents, and prepare you for taking appropriate action to address the issue, whether through HR, legal channels, or other resources.

List of Resources

This section provides a curated list of websites, organizations, and hotlines that offer support, information, and advocacy for individuals facing workplace discrimination. These resources can assist employees in understanding their rights, finding legal help, and accessing emotional support.

1. Federal Resources

- **Equal Employment Opportunity Commission (EEOC)**

  o **Website:** eeoc.gov

  o **Services:** The EEOC enforces federal laws prohibiting employment discrimination. They provide information about workplace discrimination laws, guidance on filing complaints, and resources for individuals who believe they have been discriminated against. Employees can find details on how to report discrimination, what to expect during the complaint process, and information about the rights of workers under various laws.

- **U.S. Department of Labor (DOL)**

  o **Website:** dol.gov

  o **Services:** The DOL offers resources related to labor laws, including wage and hour regulations, workplace safety, and employee rights. Employees can access information about their rights regarding pay, benefits, and working conditions, as well as links to federal labor standards.

- **Occupational Safety and Health Administration (OSHA)**

  o **Website:** osha.gov

  o **Services:** OSHA provides information on workplace safety and health, including resources for reporting unsafe conditions and discrimination related to safety violations. Employees can learn how to file a complaint regarding unsafe working environments and understand their rights to a safe workplace.

2. Legal Aid Organizations

- **National Employment Lawyers Association (NELA)**

  - **Website:** nela.org

  - **Services:** NELA is a network of lawyers who advocate for employee rights. They provide resources for individuals seeking legal assistance, including a lawyer referral service that can help employees find attorneys specializing in employment law and discrimination cases.

- **Legal Services Corporation (LSC)**

  - **Website:** lsc.gov

  - **Services:** LSC provides information about legal aid programs across the United States for low-income individuals needing assistance. They offer a directory of legal aid organizations that can help with workplace discrimination cases.

- **American Bar Association (ABA)**

  - **Website:** americanbar.org

  - **Services:** The ABA offers a lawyer referral service and resources for finding legal assistance in employment law matters. Their website includes information on how to choose a lawyer and what to expect during the legal process.

3. Advocacy and Support Organizations

- **Human Rights Campaign (HRC)**

  - **Website:** hrc.org

  - **Services:** HRC advocates for LGBTQ+ rights in the workplace and provides resources for individuals facing discrimination based on sexual orientation or gender identity. Their site offers information on workplace policies, best practices for employers, and resources for employees seeking support.

- **National Organization for Women (NOW)**

  - **Website:** now.org

  - **Services:** NOW advocates for women's rights, including workplace equality, and offers resources for reporting discrimination and harassment. They provide information on legal rights, support for victims of gender discrimination, and advocacy efforts to improve workplace conditions for women.

- **Disability Rights Education and Defense Fund (DREDF)**

  - **Website:** dredf.org

  - **Services:** DREDF focuses on disability rights, providing information and advocacy for individuals facing discrimination due to disabilities. Their resources include guidance on the ADA, information about reasonable accommodations, and strategies for asserting rights in the workplace.

4. Hotlines and Support Services

- **National Domestic Violence Hotline**

  - **Phone:** 1-800-799-SAFE (7233)

  - **Website:** thehotline.org

  - **Services:** Provides support and resources for individuals experiencing domestic violence, including workplace-related issues. They offer confidential support and guidance on safety planning and legal options.

- **Crisis Text Line**

  - **Text:** Text "HELLO" to 741741

  - **Website:** crisistextline.org

  - **Services:** Offers 24/7 support through text messages for individuals in crisis, including those dealing with the emotional impact of discrimination. Trained crisis counselors provide immediate support and resources.

- **LGBT National Help Center**

  - **Phone:** 1-888-843-4564

  - **Website:** lgbthotline.org

  - **Services:** Provides peer support and resources for LGBTQ+ individuals facing discrimination or harassment. Their services include a helpline and online resources for advocacy and community support.

5. Online Resources and Information Portals

- **Workplace Fairness**

  - **Website:** workplacefairness.org

  - **Services:** Offers a wealth of information on employee rights, discrimination, and workplace laws. This site features articles, tools for self-advocacy, and resources for understanding your rights in various employment situations.

- **Nolo**

  - **Website:** nolo.com

  - **Services:** Provides legal information and resources related to employment law, including guides on discrimination and how to protect your rights. Nolo offers self-help legal books, articles, and a directory of lawyers.

- **American Civil Liberties Union (ACLU)**

  - **Website:** aclu.org

  - **Services:** The ACLU advocates for individual rights and freedoms, including workplace discrimination protections. Their site provides educational materials on civil rights and information on how to report violations.

This comprehensive list of resources serves as a valuable tool for employees facing discrimination in the workplace, helping them find the support and information they need to navigate their rights and options. By accessing these resources, employees can take proactive steps toward understanding their rights, seeking justice, and fostering a more equitable workplace.

Sources and Recommended Reading

This section provides a curated list of sources, recommended reading materials, and relevant legislation for employees seeking to deepen their understanding of workplace discrimination, their rights, and strategies for advocacy.

1. Books

- **"Discrimination and the Law: A Comprehensive Guide" by Michael C. Harper**

    o This book offers an in-depth analysis of federal and state discrimination laws, providing case studies and practical examples.

- **"Your Rights in the Workplace: A Complete Guide to Employment Law" by Richard A. Bales**

    o A comprehensive resource for understanding workplace rights, including discrimination, harassment, and wrongful termination.

- **"The Essential Guide to Workplace Discrimination" by Elaine M. C. Wong**

    o Focused on recognizing and addressing workplace discrimination, this guide offers practical advice for employees and HR professionals.

- **"The Law of Employment Discrimination" by Robert A. Gorman and Matthew L. B. Bender**

    o A detailed exploration of employment discrimination law, including historical context, case law, and practical implications.

- **"Microaggressions in Everyday Life: Race, Gender, and Sexual Orientation" by Derald Wing Sue**

    o This book discusses the concept of microaggressions, providing examples and strategies for addressing subtle forms of discrimination.

2. Articles and Journals

- **"The Impact of Discrimination on Workplace Productivity" (Journal of Business Ethics)**

- An academic article explaining how discrimination affects employee performance and organizational culture.
- **"Understanding the Role of Employee Resource Groups in Fostering Inclusivity" (Harvard Business Review)**
  - This article discusses how employee resource groups can contribute to diversity and inclusion in the workplace.
- **"The Rise of Retaliation Claims: An Overview of Recent Trends" (Employee Relations Law Journal)**
  - A detailed examination of the increase in retaliation claims and the legal frameworks surrounding them.

3. Online Resources

- **Equal Employment Opportunity Commission (EEOC)**
  - **Website:** eeoc.gov
  - The EEOC provides resources on workplace discrimination laws, filing complaints, and understanding employee rights.
- **Workplace Fairness**
  - **Website:** workplacefairness.org
  - This site offers comprehensive information on employment rights, discrimination, and advocacy tools for employees.
- **National Employment Lawyers Association (NELA)**
  - **Website:** nela.org
  - A network of lawyers dedicated to representing employees, offering resources and support for those facing workplace discrimination.

4. Reports and Studies

- **"The Status of Women in the Workplace" (Catalyst)**
  - A research report highlighting gender disparities in the workplace, including statistics on pay equity and promotion rates.

- **"The State of Racial Discrimination in the Workplace" (Pew Research Center)**
  - o This report provides insights into the experiences of employees of color regarding discrimination and bias in various industries.
- **"Disability Discrimination in the Workplace: A National Study" (Disability Rights Education and Defense Fund)**
  - o A study examining the prevalence and impact of disability discrimination in employment.

5. Relevant Legislation

- **Title VII of the Civil Rights Act of 1964**
  - o Prohibits employment discrimination based on race, color, religion, sex, and national origin.
- **Americans with Disabilities Act (ADA)**
  - o Provides rights to individuals with disabilities and prohibits discrimination in employment, requiring reasonable accommodations.
- **Age Discrimination in Employment Act (ADEA)**
  - o Protects employees 40 years of age and older from discrimination based on age.
- **Equal Pay Act of 1963**
  - o Requires that men and women be given equal pay for equal work in the same establishment.
- **Family and Medical Leave Act (FMLA)**
  - o Provides eligible employees with the right to take unpaid leave for specified family and medical reasons.
- **Pregnancy Discrimination Act**
  - o Prohibits discrimination on the basis of pregnancy, childbirth, or related medical conditions.
- **Genetic Information Nondiscrimination Act (GINA)**

- o Prohibits discrimination based on genetic information in both employment and health insurance.

- **State and Local Anti-Discrimination Laws**

  - o Many states and municipalities have their own laws that provide additional protections against workplace discrimination.

6. Legal Aid and Advocacy Organizations

- **Legal Services Corporation (LSC)**

  - o **Website:** lsc.gov

  - o Provides access to legal aid organizations that can assist with workplace discrimination cases.

- **American Civil Liberties Union (ACLU)**

  - o **Website:** aclu.org

  - o A resource for understanding civil rights, including workplace protections against discrimination.

These sources, recommended readings, and relevant legislation will help employees gain a deeper understanding of workplace discrimination, empower them to advocate for their rights, and provide practical tools for fostering inclusivity and respect in their workplaces.

About the Author

Meet Jana Lomax, a tireless civil rights lawyer and investigator (and mom) on a mission to champion social justice and advocacy. Hailing from Kansas City, Missouri, Jana has carved out an impressive career working with various state and city civil rights agencies, where she has spearheaded hundreds of investigations into employment and public accommodations discrimination. Her extensive experience equips her with keen insights into the fight against discrimination and the pursuit of equity.

Jana brings a powerful and unique perspective to her legal work; she's Black, she's a woman, and she's the mother of child with Autism. She is deeply committed to amplifying marginalized voices and dismantling systemic barriers. Her personal journey fuels her advocacy for inclusive policies that empower individuals to recognize their rights and seek justice.

Jana's expertise encompasses a wide array of civil rights issues, and she is passionate about educating others on the critical importance of acknowledging and addressing discrimination. Through her writing and public service, she strives to inspire change and create a more equitable society for all.

When she's not advocating for justice, Jana enjoys cozy nights at home, indulging her inner foodie, diving into fantasy and thrillers—both in books and on screen—and cherishing time spent with family and friends in Kansas City, where she lives with her son.

www.ingramcontent.com/pod-product-compliance
Lightning Source LLC
Chambersburg PA
CBHW062352220526
45472CB00008B/1780